"We had taken POW's the night before.

"And we were getting ready to go into the attack on an airport and as we were getting ready to pick up and move out again we took an artillery round that landed into somewhere. I can't remember if it landed directly in front of us but out of the corner of my eye I saw a really bright unexplainable yellow flash that split second I tried to stand up. By the force of the blast I was knocked backwards and about that time I heard yelling and screaming. I looked down at my hand, when I was able to pick myself up, I was knocked back about three or four feet. I looked down at my hand and I saw blood and I couldn't see my thumb and I was scrambling through the sand looking for my thumb . . .

"I looked up and on my hand I saw my wedding ring and that's when the real fear hit me. I was thinking, 'Oh, my God, my wife. Am I ever going to miss my wife again?'"

—From the interview with
Lance Corporal
Jimmy A. Radford

DESERT VOICES

Personal Testimony from Gulf War Heroes

Lt. Commander
William H. LaBarge, USN

HarperPaperbacks
A Division of HarperCollinsPublishers

If you purchased this book without a cover, you should be aware that this book is stolen property. It was reported as "unsold and destroyed" to the publisher and neither the author nor the publisher has received any payment for this "stripped book."

HarperPaperbacks *A Division of* HarperCollins*Publishers*
10 East 53rd Street, New York, N.Y. 10022

Copyright © 1991 by William H. LaBarge
All rights reserved. No part of this book may be used or reproduced in any manner whatsoever without written permission of the publisher, except in the case of brief quotations embodied in critical articles and reviews. For information address HarperCollins*Publishers,*
10 East 53rd Street, New York, N.Y. 10022.

Cover photography by Herman Estevez

First printing: July 1991

Printed in the United States of America

HarperPaperbacks and colophon are trademarks of HarperCollins*Publishers*

10 9 8 7 6 5 4 3 2

To the men and women who fought in the Gulf War and to those who fought the war at home, but most of all to those who paid the ultimate price with their lives. America, Saudi Arabia, and Kuwait thank you for such dedicated service.

To the Armed Services of the United States of America.

To my publisher, HarperCollins, for their constant encouragement and for never doubting that I could do it.

Acknowledgments

To the men and women who participated in the interviews—without your cooperation, this book could not have become a reality.

Major Stephen C. Knechtel, U.S.A.F.—for his support during the interview stages.

Major Mark Thiffault, U.S.M.C.—for his support during the interview stages.

Ms. Celeste Warner Heymann—the manager of Tent City, who has given consistent support to this project.

Mr. Phil Kuhn—for expediting the final security clearance of the manuscript.

INTRODUCTION

On the evening of March 5th I was about to sit down to dinner when the phone rang. After the caller identified herself to the answering machine, I picked up the receiver to the sweet voice of my literary agent, Alice Martell. We engaged in some small talk before we got down to business. I knew something was up because it was almost ten o'clock New York time and Alice hardly ever called that late unless we were in negotiations for a book contract. All the deals I was involved in were completed, or so I thought.

Alice could barely hold back the news. She had talked to my publisher, Ed Breslin, who had had an idea for a book of personal testimony from Gulf War heroes, a nonfiction account in their own words of what our troops had experienced during Operation Desert Shield and Operation Desert Storm. The war was a hot topic in the publishing industry and Ed wanted to put together at speed a book of high quality to meet the rush to the bookshelves by the projects coming from competing publishers. That's where I came into the picture. Ed had been involved in the paperback publication of my national bestseller, *Sweetwater Gunslinger* 201, and he had me under contract for the novel I am currently writing, *Road to Gold*. He knew I was a veteran of the Vietnam conflict, and that I had been involved during the Iranian hostage crisis, and had also been involved in strikes against the Iranian oil platforms in the Persian Gulf. All of this made me suited for what the HarperCollins publishers had in mind for this project, now called *Desert Voices*. Ed also knew my personal motto: "I pay off on performance, not on excuses."

The deal was as follows: HarperCollins wanted me to put together a book of interviews based on the personal experiences of individuals who had fought in the Gulf War or who had been directly affected by it. I was to fly to Saudi Arabia and get the interviews from troops returning home and I was to leave as soon as possible. After Alice had fully briefed me on the proposal, the wheels started to turn. I told her I would have to get back to her once I had come up with a game plan.

The rest of the evening I spent figuring out logistics—and the probability of me actually being able to pull this off. I knew I had the leave available on the books, but the big question was whether the Navy would allow me to undertake this prestigious tasking.

That night was a restless one. I bet I got ten minutes sleep all told. I tossed and turned all night figuring out what course of action would be needed if given the green light by my commanding officer. I watched the hours approach six A.M. and when the clock struck six I hit the shower and got ready for work. I wanted to brief the C.O. before he got the morning update from the department heads at eight.

I arrived at his office a few minutes before he entered. When he opened the door, I stood up and said, "Good morning, sir. I'd like to brief you on something before your day starts."

"Sure, Sweetwater, come on in. Would you like some

coffee?"

"No, I'm fine, sir."

"What's on your mind?"

I gave him the rundown on the project and he was behind me one hundred percent except for going to Saudi. He informed me that the Navy had put out message traffic about the area being high risk and it was not advised to be visited by Department of Defense personnel. So I asked him if he would object to my meeting the troops at a halfway point, not yet knowing where that would be. He had no qualms with that course of action. He asked when I would be departing and I said as early as Monday. Before I left his office, he said that he wanted to have our legal department check on this and make sure there would be no problems or conflicts of interest on my part. I thanked him for his time and exited.

Now that everything was up front, the ball was in the Navy's court. Our legal department would check with Washington to ensure that what I was about to undertake would not be in violation of the standards of conduct and that everything was cleared before I accepted the task from HarperCollins.

During my lunch break, I called my agent to inform her of what had transpired to date. I told her it would be a go if the Navy had no objections to my doing the project and that I would know by the close of business today. I told her I would have an answer to her by nine Eastern Time tonight. At 1600 I received clearance from my commanding officer that the project had been approved.

At nine that evening I called Alice and told her the good news. I also informed her that I needed to go to Germany to conduct the interviews. She asked why Germany, and I told her why I couldn't go into Saudi. I told her that there were several stopover points being used prior to the troops entering CONUS and that I felt Germany was the best place for me to conduct my business. She told me that she would brief Ed in the morning and pass on the information, then call me at home before I left for work with more details regarding their game plan. As we finished our business, I thanked Alice for her support and belief in my capabilities in being able to make this happen.

After hanging up I realized the opportunity that was being presented to me and started to get mentally prepared for what would be a big project indeed. HarperCollins wanted the book on the streets by June 1st which was less than two months away. My wife, Nancy, could see, after I got off the phone, that I was in zone five afterburner, so she fixed me a drink and told me to sit and relax before I blew a fuse. I brought her up to speed on what had transpired to date. As I started to re-enter the earth's atmosphere, we both worked on a checklist so as not to forget anything prior to my departure. The call in the morning from Alice would clear up a lot of unanswered questions.

At seven Pacific Time, ten Eastern Time, the phone rang and Alice was ready to brief. She asked if I were awake yet, and if I wasn't, by the time she finished I surely would be. She told me that HarperCollins wanted me in New York Sunday the 10th to be briefed on the 11th and 12th and leave for Germany the afternoon of the 12th to arrive in Germany on the morning of the 13th. She said my ticket to New York would be waiting for me at the San Diego airport and a driver would meet me at JFK to take me to my hotel. I was to be at Mr. Breslin's office by ten on the morning of the 11th. The contracts, tape recorder, tapes, plane tickets and hotel reservations would all be given to me by Mr. Breslin. She then asked if I was still with her. I said keep firing and she did for another five minutes. After she answered a few of my questions I told her I would see her on Monday. She hung up and I headed for work.

There were a lot of loose ends at work that needed to be tied up before Friday. I had several projects that I was in charge of and people had to be briefed on follow-up procedures. I filled out my leave papers and hand-carried them through the chain of command once I had received my Naval investigative brief on terrorism in the European theater. By the close of business on Thursday I knew that this endeavor was real and I was playing in the Big Leagues now.

Prior to our evening meal, I was listening to the five o'clock news. It was reported that Marine troops would be returning to Camp Pendleton from the Gulf on Saturday and the public was invited to join in and welcome them home. A flash of brilliance came over me and I told Nancy we needed to be part of the welcoming committee. Besides, it would give me a chance to get warmed up before I went across the pond.

Friday morning I called Alice and told her what I was up to and asked if Ed had any guidance. She said, "Let me call him and I'll get back to you before you leave for work." Within ten minutes Alice had some guidelines for me plus a release form from the HarperCollins legal department. I gave her my fax number and she sent the form off to me.

At the close of business on Friday, I picked up a tape recorder and some tapes so that I could carry out the mission on Saturday. Nancy had picked up the release form and made 20 copies, so we were ready for our first set of interviews.

Saturday morning I was up bright and early and Nancy

had a hearty breakfast waiting when I returned from my run. We cleaned up the dishes and headed for Camp Pendleton. While driving I came up with a game plan to ensure we were up front with what we were doing.

Once on the base, I located the joint public affairs office and tracked down the officer in charge. I introduced myself as William LaBarge, explained what my mission was, and asked permission to interview the troops and their dependents. The Marine major gave me clearance to conduct my business and directed me to the parade grounds where the troops would arrive.

Nancy and I drove to the parade grounds, parked the car, and watched people file into the stands. It would be several hours before the troops actually arrived, so it gave me the opportunity to get my feet wet with a few interviews before the heroes landed.

As we watched family, friends, and patriotic bystanders file into the bleachered area, it gave one a feeling of great pride in the bringing together of our country, the likes of which hadn't been felt since World War II. Being a Vietnam veteran, I am keenly aware of the treatment accorded to the troops who served in that conflict. Our homecoming had been less than joyous. There were many instances of Vietnam veterans being jeered, or spat upon. No Vietnam veterans were met at the pier or at the airport with flags and marching bands. No one held celebrations in their honor. No one really wanted to know what it had been like. People thought they already knew. They seemed uncomfortable, uneasy, even ashamed, of what others had been asked to do on behalf of our country. There had been a great aching in the heart of America since then. Now all that was behind us. America had had the guts to do the right thing, and had succeeded in liberating Kuwait and in stopping Saddam Hussein.

This time, the welcoming home of the troops was going to be done right. The country wasn't going to let its troops down again. You could feel the sense of pride in the atmosphere. You could sense the country gluing itself together again, the returning troops transforming it. The whole scene sent goose bumps up and down my spine. People waved American flags, yellow ribbons, and banners. There was a lot of spirit.

Now that the show was underway, it was time for Jimmy Olson and Lois Lane to get some interviews. In one of the first groups I interviewed was a husband and wife whose son was returning home after being gone for seven months. As the interview progressed, the wife started to get a little emotional, which emphasized the link between a mother and her only son returning home from war.

As I strolled on the inside of the parade grounds, I spotted a man with his family sitting in the front row of the bleachers. I told Nancy that I'd bet they had someone returning, so let's talk with them. As it turned out, this man was a staff sergeant in the Marine Corps who had just returned a few days prior to this scheduled homecoming. His story was one of the most intense, eye-opening experiences of all the interviews combined. He was one of the troops who belonged to task force "Ripper" that had got pinned down in Khafji. The intensity with which he told his story made me feel like I was in battle with him. The emotional strain on him was still evident. His wife broke down during the story, my wife started to cry, and my eyes welled up. One can't imagine what it is like to be in a fire fight, but this man's story will bring you face-to-face with what it's like to be on the front line.

After that interview I needed a break. The emotional strain that was brought out in those few minutes really made you stop and think about what our men and women who serve in the armed forces go through. They are what makes this great country of ours free, and they are what the United States of America is all about.

Nancy and I got a Coke from one of the concession stands, and while we were in line, a journalist from one of the local radio stations was interviewing two gentlemen who had just returned from the Gulf. After they finished talking with this journalist, I told them what I was doing and asked if they would like to tell their stories.

Their stories brought home the real meaning of war. Both of them had been injured during the conflict. The first young man, in his early 20s, explained how he had got his hand blown off and, after he realized what had happened, had dug in the sand looking for his thumb. This young man wasn't bitter, he was proud to have served, but most of all he was glad to be alive. The other soldier had got hit in the neck with shrapnel, which had caused some nerve damage to his neck and arms. Both of these marines had met at a field hospital while they were being medically stabilized. They both had great attitudes and would go back into battle tomorrow if able. It just goes to show the courage and stamina of the American fighting forces if they know the public is behind them.

After several more interviews with people who had organized support rallies, or who had helped families having problems coping with a loved one being deployed, we went to eat dinner. The arriving troops had been delayed another couple of hours, so we took a break.

When we returned to the parade grounds, the air was charged, full of excitement—the troops were only minutes away. The mothers with newborns got to sit up front, and the children whose dads were returning were all lined up around the field with "Welcome Home" signs and banners.

As the four buses pulled into the parade gounds, the assembled crowd started to cheer and "The Marine Corps Hymn" started to blast from the loudspeakers around the field. The troops filed out of the buses and lined up into formation. The officer in charge marched them to the center of the parade grounds, gave out some instructions, then dismissed the formation. At that point all hell broke loose. Wives, children, girlfriends, mothers, fathers, and friends converged on the troops. Nancy and I sat and watched this spectacular sight in awe, and when the smoke settled, all the troops were leaving with a family member or a friend. There was someone to meet every one of the men who'd got off those buses. As for the interviews, well, it was a good thing we had had the opportunity to talk to some troops who'd arrived earlier, because there were no troops available once the dust settled.

On our drive back to San Diego, Nancy and I felt proud of our troops and could sense a coming together of the American public. All of these young troops seemed to have a mission in life, they had goals and were striving to achieve them. The younger generation that we thought had been overrun with drugs and lack of self-esteem had risen to meet the challenge of the '90s. Many of the people in the crowd at Camp Pendleton had been from out of town and had had no family members returning; they had come to witness the event and to lend their support. As I stated before, our country is experiencing a coming together, with a sense of pride and a will to succeed.

Once home I had the monumental task of packing for a two-week business trip, which I wouldn't bestow on my worst enemy. After the last item had been inventoried and packed, I hit the hay. My plane was scheduled to leave at seven the next morning, so I had a five-thirty taxi pickup.

The trip to New York was uneventful, and I relaxed once I arrived. Monday morning was busy. I met with my agent and with all the major players involved with the project. I then realized this was a reality and the monkey was on my shoulders now. It was never brought out, but I could see the strain on my agent's face and on the faces of several of the publishers as to the possibility of this project going down the porcelain fixture. I reassured them, and the tension seemed to lighten. However, I knew I might run into some unforeseen problems at my destination—and that, if I did, the project could die.

Being an optimist, I pressed on and tried to persuade everyone that I had the technology to make this happen. The rest of the day was spent getting my equipment, and confirming my tickets and reservations. It went like clockwork and the HarperCollins staff were true professionals; everything down to the last detail was covered and at my disposal.

The next day I left for Germany, where I was to meet the troops returning from Desert Storm. The flight went well and I arrived at six in the morning at my destination. I checked into my hotel and went to sleep.

At twelve noon I was awakened by my alarm. I didn't want to get out of bed, but I knew if I didn't, I would have trouble sleeping later that night. After I cleaned up, I got a taxi and headed to the base where the troops would be arriving.

Once on the base, I went to the club and got something to eat. I talked with a few people who had been involved with the war and really began to get excited about the job ahead. After lunch, I had to find the public affairs office and announce to the officer in charge what my intentions were, and get clearance to interview the troops.

After I had been briefed on the procedures for media coverage, the chief public affairs officer escorted me to Tent City and introduced me to the key players who ran the show. Tent City consisted of 58 troop tents and one large USO tent. Most of the tents had cots where the returning troops could lie down and relax while their planes got serviced for their return to the States. A couple of tents were used for administrative purposes. One was designated as the chapel, and several were designated for women only. Showers and toilet facilities were available throughout Tent City. The tents all had space heaters in them that helped keep our troops warm during the cold hours while they waited. It was quite a sight to see: the whole area was like a scene right out of the TV series "M*A*S*H*." However, the most inspirational sight in Tent City was the USO tent. It wasn't the typical drab green like the rest of the tents. This tent was white and about 60 yards long. It was like a museum inside. There were 50 state banners hung from the ceiling with yellow ribbons hanging from the bottom of each banner, and large sheets hung down as well signed by schoolchildren welcoming home the troops; there were tables laden with food and beverages for the troops to eat and drink; there was a small library of donated books, and several TVs to watch, and a Ping-Pong table to test the troops' skill. But the most historic item in the USO tent was the graffiti on the tent walls, as high up the sides as the troops could reach. There must have been hundreds of thousands of signatures and sayings all over the inside of this USO tent. For example: "Come see the Baghdad Air Show with aerial demonstrations of F-14s, F/A-18s, F-15s, F-117s, B-

52s, Tornados and the Mirage, with fly-bys by the Tomahawk cruise missile"; there were marriage proposals; there were lists of how many bombs one squadron had dropped on target; and so on and so forth, sayings after sayings after sayings. One could spend a whole day reading messages troops had written before and after going into battle. You could almost feel their emotion and pride as you read their stories. These tent walls should be put in the Smithsonian Institute as historic war memorabilia.

After I was introduced to all the key people and completed the tour of the USO tent, we went back to the headquarters tent to find out when the next planeload of returning Gulf War heroes was to arrive. The best guess they had was four-thirty that morning. I thanked everyone and asked them to call me at the hotel once the plane landed. I then headed back to the hotel to get some sleep before I started the interviews.

The hotel was only ten minutes from the base, so I could be on station within a few minutes once I received the call. After a short cab ride back to the hotel, I went up to my room and went to sleep. At ten-thirty that evening I woke up and couldn't get back to sleep, so I went down to the hotel lobby hoping to get some interviews. There I spotted three men who looked like troops just returned from the Gulf. Their haircuts, their civilian clothes and their use of English confirmed in my mind that they were military men. I went up to them, introduced myself, and explained what I was up to. They agreed to an interview, but wanted to eat first. I told them I had to get my recorder and I would be back shortly. They said they would wait in the lobby for me.

Upon my return we headed for a pub, where they could find something to eat. After several minutes of searching, we located a bar that served food. It was on the bottom floor near a rail substation. As we entered, I wondered if this would be a good place for an interview. The place was pretty loud and one of the last things Mr. Breslin said was, "Find a quiet place for the tapings." Well, when in Rome do like the Romans, and if I wanted to talk with these men I had better make the best of it. So I kept my mouth shut.

After the men had eaten, I started to interview each of them and they all had some great stories, which the tape recorder was able to pick up above the noise of the place. The emotions of one man became evident when talking about his loved ones and the hardships they had been through while he was deployed to the desert. His words were heartfelt, and touching. Two of the three men were civilian contractors who had high-tech equipment being used during Desert Storm and they needed to be on-site to ensure that it functioned properly. The ordeals they went through, and the emotional strain put on their families, were eye-opening.

Once the interviews were completed, I thanked them for their time and headed back to my hotel. Well, I thought, it wasn't going to be that easy. Almost three hours had lapsed and it was pushing two in the morning. Due to the heavy security around the airport, all the entrances to the airport's main concourse were secured. By this time jet lag had really set it and I was beaten down to parade rest. I wanted to go to bed now. Finally, after an hour of walking around who knows where, I ran into a security guard who escorted me back to the hotel entrance. I was never so happy to get into bed before in my life.

I had just entered REM sleep when the phone rang and it woke me with a start. It was the sergeant at Tent City calling to let me know that a plane had just landed with 200 troops on it who would be entering the compound within the hour. I looked at the clock and it was a quarter to five. I thought to myself: "Not bad, Sweetwater. An hour's sleep. You been there before, get a move on."

I got cleaned up and was at Tent City five minutes before the troops arrived. It was a touching sight to see. As the troops entered the USO tent, the volunteers and I all started to clap and to welcome them home. Food and drinks had been distributed prior to their arrival, so the lines had formed quickly. The troops had been on a plane for almost nine hours. They had about a two-hour layover and then another nine hours flying time to the States.

The troops looked like I felt and I am sure they felt like I looked. Once the smoke settled and the men and women got something to eat and started to relax, I went into action. I will never forget the first troop I interviewed in Tent City. He wandered over to where I was sitting and sat down several chairs away. I walked up to him and said "Welcome home," and told him why I was there and what I was up to. He agreed to an interview and I had him read the release form and sign it.

While he read the form, my heart went out to this young marine. He wasn't much more than 20 years old. His chocolate-chip camouflage desert uniform was covered with black soot and he looked like he hadn't had a shower for weeks, and you could see the emotional and physical strain on his face. As I started the interview, the young man began to cry, not from battle fatigue, but from all the excitement of going home. For him, seeing all the banners and the graffiti on the walls was overwhelming. As soon as he regained his composure, we continued and he had some great experiences to tell. Before this group's short stay was up, I had about eight good interviews. I felt good about this assignment, and I felt confident.

This was pretty much how the pattern worked while I did my research. When I knew a planeload was arriving, I would be at Tent City waiting to record our heroes' stories day or night, around the clock, for seven days. I never got more than four hours of sleep at a whack.

One day there was an antiwar demonstration outside the main gate, so the gate was secured. Fortunately, one of the USO workers got me on and off the base through a back entrance. The days were long, but the stories were breathtaking, and the troops were so proud and happy to be going home that it made the whole project worth the sacrifice.

As I went into my sixth day, the troop movement seemed to slow down and the stories were beginning to be repetitive, so I made the decision to pack my duffel and shuffle. Feeling good about what I had accomplished, I had a hidden fear of the tapes being confiscated, stolen, or erased while going through the airport X-ray machine. I hardly slept the night before returning to the States.

I had kept all the tapes in a safety deposit box at the hotel, knowing if they were lost it would hardly pay for me to go home. I felt like a CIA agent carrying hidden microfilm back through enemy lines to the Company.

The day of my departure started at six with a wake-up call and breakfast. Prior to my checkout, I got the tapes from the safety deposit box and put them in my carry-on bag, never to be out of my sight. Once I had the tapes, paranoia really set in—I couldn't afford to lose them for anything. At the airport, after checking my large suitcase, I now had only to get past the dreaded X-ray machine. As I approached the bag-eating, film-destroying, and tape-erasing monster, my blood pressure and heartbeat went off the scale.

As I got in line to send my bag through, I took all the tapes out and put them in a large envelope. I told the lady checking tickets that I had tapes in the envelope, and asked if she would mind handing them to me once I had cleared the machine. She gave a friendly smile and said "Sure," after she had checked the contents of the envelope. Once on the other side, I was home free. The only way these tapes would not be delivered now was if the plane went down or I was shot.

The trip home was long and I couldn't wait to get these hot potatoes off my hands. Once I cleared customs, my driver was waiting to take me to the hotel. After checking in, I called Mr. Breslin's office and talked to his lovely assistant, Laurie van Rooten, who, by the way, had set up my flawless travel arrangements. I told Laurie I would be in to debrief and turn in the tapes as soon as I got cleaned up. She welcomed me home and said she would relay the message once Mr. Breslin returned.

The debrief, and turning over the tapes, was a big relief, a load off my shoulders. It was like getting back aboard the aircraft carrier at night with a 20-foot pitching deck in a rainstorm. The debrief went well and everyone seemed pleased with the results, so we secured for the day. The following day, the publishing team and I laid out the game plan for the birth of *Desert Voices*.

As you read this book, bear in mind that during the interviews, I would often prompt the interviewee with questions, many times because I myself was so excited by what was being said, other times because something being said wasn't quite clear enough, and still other times because the subject of the interview was having trouble finding words in such a highly charged state. My questions have been eliminated and the stories have been smoothly stitched together. The publishers and I wanted to keep the spotlight on the troops, to let them tell their own stories of what the war in the Gulf was really like. Many memoirs of war have been published, but mostly by generals, and we wanted to let the troops have their memoirs preserved, and in their own words. If there is any military terminology you don't understand, turn to the glossary in the back.

As I sat on the plane home to San Diego, I could not believe all that had been accomplished in so few days. I only hope you enjoy reading these accounts of war by our brave men and women of the armed forces as much as I was honored to gather them for you—and for posterity.

William LaBarge
San Diego, California
April 8th, 1991

JIMMY A. RADFORD

Rank: Lance Corporal
Service: Marine Corps
Duty: Infantry
Hometown: Paradise, California

We were the first ones in the Third Battalion Seven Marines, we were the first ones into Kuwait. You know the night of the 25th as we were clearing buildings we took artillery fire and me and five other Marines were wounded. One was killed. And from there they medivacked us down into Jabal into Frankfurt, Germany, and we arrived in here yesterday at Camp Pendleton.

I lost part of my hand. Artillery shrapnel had taken part of the hand off and then what they could save of it was saved and sewed on and then I got six to eight months of physical rehabilitation at Camp Pendleton. There's nerve damage and I had lost part of my hand, a little bit of my hand. I got I guess what you call a superficial face wound, lost a lot of skin, a lot of nerve tissue, everything and then the rest will be a, through, uh, surgery. Will be refaced.

It's not serious to me 'cause I'm home and I'm alive and that's why it's not serious, you know, and pretty soon I'll be able to be with my wife again and then our first child's due in July so that's basically why I'm not worried about anything.

There's about ten seconds there that, uh, the biggest fear in my life was I was worried. Once everybody knew, once I knew everything was okay and I was all right then I really felt okay.

We had taken POWs the night before. And we were getting ready to go into the attack on an airport and as we were getting ready to pick up and move out again we took an artillery round that landed into somewhere. I can't remember if it landed directly in front of us but out of the corner of my eye I seen a really bright unexplainable yellow flash that split second I tried to stand up. By the force of the blast I was knocked backwards and about that time I like heard yelling and screaming. I looked down at my hand, when I was able to pick myself up, I was knocked back about three or four feet, I looked down at my hand and I seen blood and I couldn't see my thumb and I was scrambling through the sand looking for my thumb.

In the process of that, I looked up and on my hand I seen my wedding ring and that's when the real fear hit me. I was thinking, "Oh, my God, my wife. Am I ever going to miss my wife again?" And we are expecting our first child to be born in July, on July 23rd and the thoughts going through my head was, "My wife. What if my child was, you know, I'll never be able to see my child. My child will never be able to see me," and those thoughts of fear were going through me then.

That was when a corpsman ran up to me, when my best friend was saying that I was hit, I was hit. My corpsman ran up to me and was able to grab a hold of me and look at me real quick. I said, "I'm okay, I'm okay." And I said, "I'm all right, I'm all right, go help the other guys," and he ran over to help the more serious wounded and everything. My buddy was helping me out, he bandaged my hand up and we were expecting more incoming and everything.

I'll probably be going for a six-to-eight month therapy depending on the extent of the nerve damage done and everything and what they determined so far was bruise nerves inside the thumb through my fingers to the knuckles of the fingers are bruised. The damage to the nerves caused my hand to stay at a point where it's constantly swollen all the time, where I can't pull my ring off, the ring won't come off and at this first aid station I put up a hell of a fight. They wanted to cut my ring off and I wouldn't let them. I told them my wife put that on there and it's going to stay there no matter what happened.

The field medics were the greatest we've ever had. The corpsmen, the Navy corpsmen nowadays, I don't care what anybody says about Marines or what the Marines say about the Navy. The corpsmen are the best damn people we have out there with us because we rely in a situation like that we're so busy shooting, we're getting shot and somebody's shooting back that we need them to be running around and helping us, helping our wounded, and they also get up and help them firefight and they've got balls.

I felt very confident. We practiced for months out there in the desert just for this one attack we were going to do. We arrived in the country January 14th. We were slated for contingencies in the Orient, in the Phillippines, and then we were preparing for about a month and half before we went over for the deployments to the Saudi. And then once in country we basically knew what our mission would be and so we had two months to rehearse the facts of the mission and everything and once we went in, we were unstoppable.

ROBERT S. EDWARDS

Rank: Staff Sergeant
Service: Marine Corps
Duty: Communications
Hometown: Oceanside, California

Well, when we first flew in, we flew into Dhahran on August the 11th. It was nine o'clock at night. It was 115 degrees when we pulled into the airport. Of course, everybody was tired. From there, once we all got together, we moved down to a port called Jabal Port where everybody lived and slept in warehouses. And we slept on the concrete. Warehouses—there was about, I'd say, 800 people in a warehouse. No beds, no nothing. We just slept on the concrete and that's how we lived.

When we first got there, there was no shower facilities for about a week. From there, I was picked to go with the combat service support unit up to the front. And at that time, it was in early August, we left and went up to the desert and we supported the grunt units that was up front, the ground units. When we first moved out we was the northernmost American unit in the Saudi desert. From there, we moved further north as time progressed. And everything was really peaceful at first until, I guess, oh, about four or five months ago.

About four months ago, we moved up, I guess we was about 50 miles from the border on our first move and we started getting reports of them coming across the border probing artillery shells and rockets. As things progressed, we moved up even closer to the border, near Khafji. Then we started getting artillery fire, incoming rockets. A lot of the people over there were in my section, in my platoon, had most of my men, well, I was the oldest person in my platoon. I'm 31. And most of the men in my platoon were between the ages of 19 and, I'd say, 24 and you become, you just come to know everybody living with them, living in a hole all the time and they get scared.

'Course, I was scared too, but we all learned to kind of pull together as a big family and just overcome that fear. When a SCUD attack would come or we'd get warning of a SCUD attack, everybody would be in a panic and they'd run into their bunkers and they'd just crouch there. Some of the guys, and I don't mind saying, some of the guys cried. Some of them, you know?

They cried, but I tried to hold them together even though I myself was scared. I had 20 men under me. I'm with the communications platoon and what we would do is we would have bulldozers go in before we moved into a position and because the desert is so flat and barren, what they would do is the bulldozers would dig a trench about eight-foot deep into the ground and we would drive our communications vehicles down in them and that's where we would keep our vehicles and then we would dig slit trenches that would be, let's say, about 12-foot long and about three-foot wide at the most and that's where we would go when an attack would come or when we got closer to the border we lived in them trenches most of the time.

We had a couple people that was bitten by desert vipers, sand vipers, snakes, and they were rushed out to the hospital. Scorpions. We seen a scorpion and this is the truth: I seen a scorpion that was about, I'd say, six inches long from tail to head and it was solid black in color and there was a couple people that were bit by them. The food. We got one hot meal a day and that was usually in the evening and some of the times, by the time it got to us, it was already cold anyhow. But it was better than eating rations.

I think that the troops knew what was going on because we were told, the staff NCOs and the officers were told not to hide anything from the troops. That if we knew it, and my policy, personally, was that if I knew it I was telling the troops so they'd be informed. Now, as communicators, we usually knew what was going on before anybody else anyhow 'cause we'd hear it come over the radio and I usually spread the word and let everybody know what was going on just to keep them informed.

We went into Khafji for resupply and for LAVs to resupply them with ammunition. Light armored vehicles. They got, pretty much got trapped in there because when the tanks come across—see I'm not sure what was told over here, but when the tanks came across, they had the turrets turned and the Saudis was up in front of us. And that's an international sign of surrender. So the Saudis let them come through. Well, once they got down to Khafji, and there was no one in the city of Khafji, it'd been evacuated since we started the ground, or the campaign over there, they turned the turrets back around.

And we were kind of caught, but then the Saudis moved around behind them and we had them cut off. They couldn't get out. So it was more or less, I think that's why they fought as hard as they did was because they were cut off. They couldn't go nowhere so they started battling and the Marines were there for, I think, let's see, a day and a half is actually when the Marines were in there, in Khafji. We were kind of strangled off in there, couldn't get out because of the fire, but we pulled out and because the Saudis wanted to go into Khafji and take it back because it's their country so the Marines pulled back to the rear and used supporting fire and artillery and aircraft to cover the Saudis while they went in and liberated it again.

I think it was two days of hard battle, yeah. And there were still some stragglers that was held up in the buildings, but the Kuwaitis, 'scuse me, the Saudis went in and did a door-to-door and took 'em all out.

The problems that we had with our equipment and our weapons was just a problem of getting used to the desert and the environment. Once we got used to it, and, you know, after our first couple months we was there, things started working out. We learned how to adapt and overcome a lot of the problems and get around them and work around the problems and there was no real major problems over there and our equipment—there's no doubt in my mind that our equipment is much better than any equipment they had over there.

They didn't want to fight. They didn't have the heart. They wasn't into it. I think, actually, and this is just me, I feel compassion for the people because you gotta feel sorry for them. They were forced to be there, they didn't want to be there and when you see 'em come out crying and begging you because they thought that we would kill them once they surrendered because that's what they were told, you have to feel compassion for the people.

The ones that I seen were—some of them didn't have shoes, their clothing was probably been soiled for weeks on end. It was tattered. They had body lice. Sores on their bodies. They were in bad shape.

Before we went in, we could hear the bombs being dropped. Not only could we hear them, but we could feel it. I mean the earth shook. When the B-52s came in and they started doing their bombing runs, the earth would shake even on the other side of the border back in to Saudi Arabia, you could feel the earth shake. They started dropping what they call Daisy Cutters. They're 15,000-pound bombs. When they drop them, I thought for sure that we had been hit because the earth, you could actually stand in your trench and looking out you could actually see the earth move up and down in front of you. And you could feel the camouflage netting that we had over the holes, the cami netting would go in and out. It would fluctuate in and out, you could actually feel it.

You know, being with communications I'd been in the ground units almost my whole 14 years I been with ground units and I've always said things about air wing and pilots—oh, they got the easy life, this and that—tell you what, I'll never, ever talk bad about pilots again because if it wasn't for them, we would have never been able to do what we did. They was the key to the whole thing. And I want to get back to work and get back with my people and try to get all the gear back and get it all in order and just, I kind of want to be with them, around them, right now.

Emotionally, when the SCUD attacks first started, emotionally for everybody it was a roller coaster. We could get word over the radio, "SCUD has been launched," and no one knew in which direction or where it was going and all we knew is that he had chemical capabilities and the first time we got the SCUD launched, everybody went to MOP level four in their chemical suits which means we put the whole suit on, mask and everything, and there was people that was running. There was people that was crying. You know, it was just mass confusion. And then everytime you'd get a SCUD attack your heart would race, your adrenaline would go up and you'd just say this was the one. This was the one. And then after a couple of months, it was just, "SCUD attack," okay, no big deal. Nobody really worried about it anymore. We just went, sat in the trench and just waited for the all clear.

I was surprised because we were told that HE was going to use chemical weapons, that he had the capability and he would use them. But we were also told by some POWs that one of the reasons that he didn't come down as much onto the Marine Corps side with his troops was because his troops were told, they were deathly afraid of us. They were told for some reason that the Marines, in order to get into the Marine Corps and to be a Marine, to show your faith to the Marine Corps you had to kill a family member. That's what Saddam had told his troops and so they were deathly afraid. That's why they surrendered to the Egyptians and they were afraid to surrender to the Marines because they were told that we would peel their skin off, we would kill them, we'd do terrible things

So they were deathly afraid of us and they told us that when we got POWs. I'm sure you seen, I seen some photos on CNN where they was kissing the Marines' hands and their feet and begging them not to kill them. That's what they were told, you know. And, of course, that's not true because none of our people treated them that way. When we took POWs, we took care of them. But you feel that in your heart because you see 'em and you can't help but feel sorry for 'em.

To be honest, when we first heard about Iraqi planes landing in Iran, we thought that maybe Iran was going to get involved and maybe they were going to help 'em out. And then we were being told that no, that Iran told 'em that they couldn't have any of the aircraft back. And once

General Schwartzkopf came on and told us that, hey, they're not getting them back, we know what they're doing. You know, we felt better 'cause it was kind of comic that even though we were marines and General Schwartzkopf was in the Army that man—everybody kind of looked up to him because he was like the hero of the whole thing. Even the allies looked up to him. He was the man of the whole thing.

Even, I'll say as far back as 90 to 100 miles from the border into Saudi Arabia in the daytime, say at 12 noon, it would be black. The sky would be black. It be dark outside. It'd look like it was fixing to storm and it was just smoke from the oil fields. Every night, you could smell it more than you could during the day because the winds was up during the day. But at night you could smell this burning oil smell. Matter of fact, it almost made you sick to your stomach because it was so thick in the air. And you could smell it and it got on your skin and you could rub your skin like that and black would come off. Just a oily black. The oil in the air.

You know it was the Far East Network, it seemed like that was one of the things they was playing more than anything, that was the protest. And that started making people mad. The men that was over there. They started getting mad. And the way I look at it is, it disgusts me and makes me mad but everybody has their own right to an opinion and that's what we went over there to fight and to give them that right, to voice their own opinion and even though I don't agree with it, I'd do it all again, today, to give everybody that right.

And when we started getting these Any Serviceman letters, and they would come in and they would be like—

let's say the helicopters would drop off our mail and there'd be maybe 40 bags of mail there for our unit. And 20 bags of it would be Any Serviceman letters. That's when we started feeling it. When we started knowing we were supported. And we would write these people back and they would write us and like at Christmas time they sent us boxes—of food. They sent us presents. They sent us, I mean anything. They just—people we never knew. They sent us all kinds of stuff. That's when we started realizing.

Everybody, you know, everybody was telling us we all, you know, the real warriors were the ones that fought at World War II, at Guadalcanal in the South Pacific and this and that and the other. Vietnam, you know, we lost that war and this and that and the other. But the big difference here was that General Schwartzkopf and all his field commanders ran that war. They did what they wanted to do. They told the president what was going on and the president stayed back and said, "Okay, is that what you want to do?" And it made a lot of difference. I mean, he ruled that with a iron glove and sometimes he was very blunt with people. He got what he wanted and it came out for the better for everybody.

I think the main POW that we heard about and the first one we heard about was Jeffrey Zahn and my brother-in-law who was over there with me plus two cousins and an uncle, my brother-in-law's last name is Zahn and he's from New Jersey and he has a cousin that is in the Navy. So the first thing that I thought and the first thing that my brother-in-law thought was—'cause all we knew was Zahn was the last name and it was a pilot—was that his brother-in-law had been taken POW. I was mad because my brother-in-law was upset and he was mad. And then I started thinking about it and then we found out it wasn't him and I was just mad because that they took him and we heard that they was doing, they was beating him or they had showed pictures and we had heard that the pictures showed, made him look like he had been beaten and everybody was outraged. And they wanted to go, why can't we go now, let's do it now and the field commanders said, in due time. We'll wait. We'll do this at the right time.

At first we was upset because we felt like everything's going to be done by Air and we'd set here for almost seven months and we haven't and we're not going to get a chance to go in and prove ourselves 'cause we felt, I know most of the people that I was with felt like they owed something to the United States to prove that we were still what everybody thought we were. And that we could still do it. And as the air war progressed and went on and on, everybody's opinion started changing and they started saying, "Wait a minute. Why don't we let 'em do as much damage as they can before we go in." 'Cause we started thinking about how many people would be lost if we went in. And everybody kind of just calmed down and set in for the long run and waited.

And once it kicked off. . . . We was on a four-hour notice. We had been on a four-hour notice for some time. And what they would do is say, "Okay, in four hours everything has to be packed and moving 'cause we're going to go and move in." We knew where our assembly areas were. We knew what we would do. We had already been briefed. We knew what everything was going to go on. We had rehearsed it over and over and over as to how we were going to do it. We knew what our objectives were. Once it kicked off, it was like a big pressure being lifted. 'Cause you knew this was the time, this was time. And at first everybody just kind of looked at each other, you know, with this amazed look like, "Oh no, it's really going to happen."

And then after things started moving, everybody just, they just all snapped together. Everything was together and people just started moving and motivation was high. I mean, everybody wanted to go in and they wanted to kick ass. Everybody was ready to go, you know. "Let's go, let's do it!" They wanted to keep on pushing.

But we had been told that there was a great possibility that once we had launched the ground campaign and started that everybody on the other side, that the Iraqis would say, would surrender in masses. We had been told that that was a great possibility because that is a way that the Arab nation, that a lot of them do that. They surrender in masses when they surrender. And, sure enough, they was coming out. That's it, they don't want none. They don't want to fight. Some of the more elite units would put up a token fight. They'd fire a few shots off and then white flags would go up and they'd come out.

At that point in time there's probably a million thoughts racing through your mind. Your family, your friends, everyone that's around you, your job. Everything's going through your mind at one time and you just, you try to sort out what you should be concentrating on, what you should be thinking about. I don't know, it's hard to explain. There's a thousand thoughts going through your mind at one time.

We didn't know about the commanders. We were told that they had, we were told that they had death squads from Hussein's elite. That anybody who tried to surrender they were going through and killing them. We knew this and that's when they started the leaflet campaign and started dropping leaflets telling 'em to surrender, that they'd be taken care of, that they would be all right once we had 'em. We would take care of them and protect 'em and so forth and that's when we started seeing them. They started coming across the border. Some of them that we got were wounded from coming through the minefields. One Iraqi had his foot blown off and he still made it to surrender. You know they lost a lot of 'em trying to surrender, but they were afraid to go back north because they were afraid that they would be killed.

The intelligence and the pilots and from photos we knew basically where the minefields were, ranging from, some of them stretched, I'd say, about 90 to 100 miles across. And they'd be 60 meters in depth to 600 meters in depth. And there was two large minefields that we knew about where we were going to breach at and we were told about them, too, and there was 20 kilometers in between each of the minefields. We knew about them. They were laid with, I mean, they knew what they was doing when they laid them minefields. But there was an assortment of mines in there. We were told up to 400,000 mines in one strip, you know, of mines, covering from antipersonnel to gas mines to tank mines, anything you can think of they had in there.

Before they get that cleaned up over there, that's going to be a long time. The biggest thing is going to be the fires. It's going to take them years to put that out.

Once we started seeing the air campaign and we started hearing about what the air campaign was doing and we knew then that it was going to be very short. But we were told once the ground campaign started, that if it lasted past the month, to be prepared for a long haul. 'Cause it was going to be a long time, that we would be there for a long time if the ground campaign went further than a month. But once we started seeing what the pilots were doing and what the aircraft could do, we had no doubts in our mind anymore, we knew that it was going to be short.

Every time we see a plane go over we give 'em, "Go get 'em!" 'Cause we knew that they was really tearing them up 'cause we was hearing the report and of course over the radio I was hearing the things that was coming over and it was like, "I can't believe this. These guys are wasting 'em." It was a lot of dissension among the different services, but after things started going and clicking together everybody became a big family and there was, I know in like your own personal unit, or your own platoon, there probably isn't nothing that I don't know about any man in my platoon. I know how many of 'em's married, I know which ones had children, I know which ones have girlfriends, I know—it's just 'cause we talked all the time. We was like a big family. We just became a family. Together.

I originally went over with BS's G-70 unit that's coming back today and then after things started going I was attached to Task Force Ripper. I was with Task Force Ripper. It's just the designator, it's the name of the task force that I was with which was compiled of Seventh Marines, Fifth Marines, First Tanks, Combat Engineers, LAVs. It was a mechanized task force with ground support units. Ground units. And as you probably seen they went, I mean, Task Force Ripper pushed all the way through and took the Kuwait airport which they had a battle at the Kuwait airport but they never stopped. They constantly pushed, they knew what they was doing. We rehearsed it over and over and over until everybody could do it in their sleep.

There was, you know, there was people, what people don't think about it is when you're moving that many people, that many vehicles, and different types of vehicles, some vehicles because of the gear ratio have to run at a certain speed and others have to run at another speed. Well, this causes a fuel problem and then you have to say, "Okay, we're going to give these fuel now, we're going to give these fuel this time," and in others words, a big logistics problem and it was like it all worked out smooth because the guys that was in charge of the logistics just they knew what to do, they did it and I'm telling you, people are going to be studying this for years to come on how they did this, because it's amazing.

JEFFREY M. ALLISON

Rank: Sergeant
Service: Army
Duty: Tanker
Hometown: Ellenville, New York

My unit deployed, actually, it was just four platoons out of my battalion, one from each line company. We went down to Saudi Arabia, we arrived in Saudi Arabia on the 14th of February. I'm in a tank command, the M1A1s. The big 120s. What we did is we were part of a core of reserves, as replacements, if it was necessary. And my particular platoon actually got a mission to go with another unit, which was an MI unit.

You stay with your vehicles. With tankers, it depends on what kind of rotations you've got with security. And with the missions that we had when we were out there, you stayed with the vehicle. But when we were part of the replacement organization, we stayed in tents.

As a matter of fact, once my platoon was forward deployed with this MI unit, that's Military Intelligence. It's a contradiction, but I think—we were allowed to do some patrolling up along the tri-border with Iraq, Kuwait and Saudi Arabia, along the berms that they had along there. And at one time, we had fifteen EPWs surrender to us.

These guys were in better shape than the others that we had in the little camp we had set up for it in our base. We had a—what was it, 287 of them, come in at night time. We had to set up a little concertina wire perimeter with the little platoon of infantry that we had up there that was attached to MI also. And we guarded them overnight and into the next day. They all had left their weapons. Supposedly it was an infantry company that we was guarding, and they had a tank gate in front of them which got overran, and apparently they said that they left their weapons where they were in the bunkers. And they walked across about 80 K's.

They were poorly clothed. I'd say that a quarter to one third of them had no shoes or socks. It was very chilly at night, the temperature probably dropped, let's say, anywhere from twenty to thirty degrees.

Because of us being a security element, we were not allowed to patrol that deeply into Iraq with the minefields. But we've seen some of the barriers and stuff that was along the border area. I believe the Saudi government had put up the berm system. There was a major berm that ran all along the tri-border area. And supposedly it was to stop armored vehicles.

A berm is a massive—it's basically a pile of dirt, sand, rocks, whatever you might have to form a wall. Basically, it's set up and designed to stop any large vehicles.

As far as the minefields, all I can do is speculate on accounts that I have heard, because like I say, we didn't —weren't allowed to patrol that far north to even get close to them. But just from seeing accounts and hearing things from the group of infantry that was with us, because they did do some things, and they scouted forward. Basically, they found the mines and they marked them. They basically knew where everything was.

In the tank, I'm a gunner. On the M1, I have at my disposal a 120 millimeter smooth bore cannon. I can shoot an armored-piercing sabo round, or I can fire a heat-seeker which is a high explosive anti-tank round. 4,000 yards is pushing it. We prefer something in closer to 3200 or less. We use CVC's, so everybody is communicating with everybody in the vehicle. You must work as a group.

With the new M1A1 it's got the NBC defense system, so if you run it with an overpressurization system, it naturally sends filtered air through, so you can use that as a cooling system. There's four crew members. The tank commander or TC, he has the basic overall responsibility for the vehicle. That is on most cases, such as a platoon sergeant and the wingman tanks with the platoon leader's vehicle. The platoon leader, he's got a lot of things going on in his mind, so the crew has to be stacked. He's got the cream of the crop out of his platoon. So everybody knows what they're doing, everybody's doing their job, and basically, it is up to the gunner to run things when the fighting comes. The TC's too busy communicating with the platoon and with us.

I've developed a system where I do work with the driver. Me and him, we click together. His job tells him where he has to go. This particular crew, we've only been together since last June. And we've been through two gunneries, and that's as a matter of fact is when we got a brand-new lieutenant.

Surprisingly enough, what the critics were saying before the war did not really affect us. They were saying that the vehicles were breaking down every fifteen or twenty minutes. We ran into no problems. The only thing that we had to worry about is, because with the turbine engine, it sucks a lot of air into the system, and it's got very big air filters and pre-cleaners. So once we go out on a mission, we come down, we must stop and do maintenance for about a half-hour, cleaning air filters.

If it goes beyond our maintenance level, yes, there's ways. With a regular unit, you know, they have mechanics there that are specifically trained for that type of vehicle. Any crew is interchangeable between vehicles.

Prior to the ground offense starting, it was interesting, I was on guard one night, and I sat there and watched on the horizon what turned out to be a B-52 strike. You see in the distance, on the horizon, just massive flashes of white and yellow and orange light. And it just continues. It's like a strobe light blinking, but it's continuous.

There were several that we watched, and it's hard to even tell, because you're not paying attention to time. And then after a while the sound and the shock wave of it comes to you, even being that far away. You could feel the shock waves.

We slept on our vehicles. It depended, at night, what shifts or what you had, type of security, that night. If you used—if you didn't have to move our turrets at all, there's plenty of flat surface to sleep on the vehicle. I personally hate sleeping on the ground.

Logistics worked surprisingly well. All you had to do was put in the request through your chain of command, and the operations basically set it up. We always had fuel, always. With the mission that we had, we was at one central location. So basically we had our mission for the security for an airfield, and we stayed there, and when fuelers would come in they would allow us to go out and come back. We definitely knew how far we could go. I know it's over 400 gallons of fuel. It's a multi-fuel system, but we do run on diesel. JP-8 can be used. It's just the hotter the level that you get, the less they like it, because of the different flash points.

With the possibility of un-knowing of SCUD attacks—because as soon as we got in country, several hours later, we had a SCUD attack. And then later that night, we were just sleeping, about one or two in the morning, and somebody would come in and wake you up out of a dead sleep, yelling "SCUD attack!" I did see three of them get shot down. By Patriots. It happened so quick. The Patriot, I guess, right after launch, hits Mach 2, which is twice the speed of sound. And it goes up and it just—I mean, it's within the proximity of it, and it just blows it out of the sky.

All you basically hear is a boom when it hits the speed of sound. And then you see the explosion. It's over that quick. A little unnerving.

Prior to going over there, we was constantly watching the news, you know, and everything, and every now and then they would show that. What little war protesters there was, we all knew—you know, you can also see that they also started showing the support. They showed the president running around, and the vice president running around. And just people calling home and talking to families, knowing there's yellow ribbons all over the towns. And it was very—it was a good idea, you know. It made you feel good. I've really got nothing planned at all. I'm just going to go home, relax. It's been three years since I've been home.

Once we got back in country, which was just this past Friday, we took a little bit of time off, and then we had leave forms waiting for us, because the rest of my battalion is deployed right now. I guess they figured we had enough time down there so we didn't have to shoot this time. We'd already gone through two gunneries already in the past year. So people who wanted leave took leave, and those who wanted to go home were allowed to go home.

Gunneries force is where the tank crews go out and they qualify with their weapons systems, with the tank.

And you go through several different tables, training up to a qualification table, which is Table Eight. And then you go through a couple of other tables higher, which is like a section gunner, which is one vehicle and his wing man. And another level higher which is the platoon level, where you have a whole platoon of our vehicles.

I didn't have a chance to work with the coalition forces, although I've talked with a different, a few of them out there, because they're all interested, you know, everybody gets to work together, and they're really interested in working together. Just brief meetings with, you know, Egyptian forces. The Saudi forces. I've seen some service, I guess they were either Red Cross or just some— I'm not sure what kind of service they were, from Poland, a team from Czechoslovakia. And this was all down at KK&C, which is the Saudi military complex.

They had run recons along the border the whole time, expecting EPWs, and they brought in the 287 prisoners. So they brought them in and they put them in this little camp. And it was just something for us to watch overnight. They didn't even know we were there until first light in the morning, and they see these tanks looking— and all the gun turrets pointing at them. It really shocked them pretty good. Like, you don't have to point that at us any more, we're friendly, we surrendered. *(Laughs.)*

But the interesting side story to it was that one of the guards here had an M-16, and he didn't have ammo in it, but he had the bolt to the rear, and he set it down butt first. With an M-16, if you do that, the bolt is going to snap forward, and he then about broke a couple of necks over there when that bolt snapped forward, and they snapped—look—looking. They thought we'd fed them their last meal the night before, we fed them MREs. The people were so hungry! I mean, we took out all the pork and ham ones because, you know, it has something to do with religious beliefs or something like that. But they would open the meal pack and licked the insides of them. And when we got in with them the next day, a good percentage of them didn't have any shoes or socks. We went into our own bags, because we had brought PT gear, our own personal stuff, and gave them sweats, our sneakers, we gave them socks. Just different things to help them stay warm. I mean, it was crazy. It was just . . . I don't know, you do what you can do to help them. It's not their fault.

Mostly the whole group came as a company, I guess, and there was a few in there that wouldn't accept the clothing. They were Saddam this and Saddam this, and Saddam is great. And their ExO talked with one of the people that was in the group there that translated from Arabic, and basically he told him that these people are giving you clothes off their backs, clothes of their own personal stuff, and you're turning them down? He called him some not nice words back, but, you know.

We had a little booklet out, and supposedly the Republican Guard had a type of red triangular or diamond patch, I can't remember exactly any more, that distinguished them from the rest. The Republican Guard, it was their—they were a little bit better people, they got fed, they had the uniforms. These people had uniforms, but some of them were not standard, they had like . . . Soviet-type MOS gear, and some of them just had brown, you know, green pants, any type of uniforms they probably could have got their hands on. Some of them were wearing civilian jackets. One guy was wrapped up in a parachute to help himself stay warm. It was just a piece of white nylon he had wrapped around himself.

I can't imagine myself being on the other side, being pounded for a month by the Air Force like that. Not every day, hour after hour. I can't picture it. The infantry that was with us were allowed to do some reconnaissance into the military—and they brought back a lot of things. A lot of weapons, like AK-47s, with the wood stocks that were dry-rotted, falling apart. Things like that. They brought back a lot of equipment. It was just left there. Just left.

Nobody was in any of the bunkers that they went through. It was really something. Well, you did have occasions—I did hear the one story where people did go in there and there was still people there. It was something else. I still can't get over the people, their soldiers. 80 K's in no shoes or socks. People's feet were swelled. Unbelievable. We had medics there that were treating them, you know, on an individual basis. And there was one actually sick enough that they had to put a cot in there and he stayed on that and they took him out on that cot when the buses came to pick them up.

ANDREW G. DIDCOCT

Rank: Lance Corporal
Service: Marine Corps
Duty: Artillery
Hometown: Birmingham, Alabama

I got to Saudi Arabia August 17. It was very hot. They put us at the port for a week waiting for our gear and I remember the heat that seemed to never let up. They put us in big warehouses and there was no breeze and the security was real tight. We had armed guards everywhere and they had live rounds. It was basically pretty boring.

I'd say it was about 120. We drank probably two, three gallons a day. 'Course they set up showers, portable showers, the Navy did and everybody go out there. I took two, three showers a day just to cool down. When I was over there I was with Headquarters 311. That's artillery. I was a radio operator. I would work in the batallion FDC and copied down message traffic and fire missions and also worked on antenna hill and that's responsible for the maintenance and to make sure the com stays up.

Com was excellent. It was actually better there than over here in the States 'cause the land was so flat. The problem we had, most of the antennas the temperature would get so hot you would touch the antenna it would burn your hands and the mast sections they go about 30, 40 feet in the air, they actually welded themselves together. So we had, we couldn't break them down, so we had to tie them to the sides of vehicles. We had to improvise, we did a lot of things over there we normally didn't do over here.

When we first got there, we start up probably about 60 miles from the Kuwait border. And they brought bulldozers and they dug huge holes, big enough to park the vehicles in. And we put the camie nets on top and we slept on the ground. We dug fighting holes around the perimeter and set up security, but actually we just slept on the ground and we got caught about November.

We had a, you know, a lot of scorpions. Some guys were bit by scorpions. But snakes. I saw one snake one marine had killed. The scorpions, they mostly, if you left your gear on the ground, on the deck, they like to get inside your gear, so if you picked up your flak jacket, your helmet, you had to make sure to shake it out. And every time we'd dig a fighting hole, we'd run into them. There was a lot of bugs. We'd call them, we called them shit bugs, because if you go out there and dig a shitter and you could hear them inside the hole. They sound like crickets. And they were everywhere.

For a while we just used, we made showers. Get 5 gallon water jugs and we would build a little portable shower and just unscrew the top and let it come on you, and then for about a month they had a dragon wagon. And they had portable showers on the back. It's an LVS, it's a big tractor trailer looks funny, looks like a moon. Marine Corps had them. I don't think the Army has them.

When we first got there we had, everybody was real nervous about gas and SCUD attacks. They told us we were in range of their SCUDs, but we had two or three SCUD attacks when the air war started. When they started firing the SCUDs we'd run to our holes but, hell, I only went two or three times but after that we didn't have any more. Most of our news came from the armed forces network 'cause we were really cut off out there and sometimes we'd improvise antennas and we pick up other places had SCUD attacks. Actually we were in a good spot, we weren't up front and we weren't in the rear. We were in between.

I could hear the bombing and I could see the flashes of light and there were always planes, there were always helicopters and planes. We knew what was going on. I remember what happened. It was like 3:30 in the morning. I was asleep and I was on antenna hill working and they called up and said we need to bring two more nets up so I did, hook up two more radios and I woke everybody up. I said, "Hey, bombing started," and everybody's going back to sleep.

Everybody. We'd been out there such a long time and had been through so much that it seemed, people back home are stressing out a lot more than we were. We were actually, even during the war, during the supposedly gas attacks and all these other things. I thought we were very calm.

I just got off a six-month float where I went to the Philippines, Thailand, Korea, Hong Kong, Singapore. And we had trained in Twenty-Nine Palms for several weeks so we were ready. I just had to get climatized. That was the big thing. Actually during the day we would, they would let us, we had a rotation system working like six on twelve off and during the day we wouldn't even work. We'd work in the mornings, the afternoons they'd leave us alone 'cause it was just too hot. Everybody would build shelters and you'd fall asleep you'd wake up you'd get a headache your mouth would be real dry. So you'd try to sleep at night.

The winter was different. What happened, the condensation would get real bad on the nets and you'd wake up in the morning you'd think it would be raining but the nets would be dripping and the weapons would rust and your gear would get all wet, but it got very cold. They shipped some cold weather gear, some long johns, and the British, we had some British cold weather gear and that helped a lot. But it got very cold.

We cleaned them every day. We had COP. Clean or Lubricant Protected. And we had rifle cleaning gear. And we had to clean it and dust it down and we would wrap it, a lot of people would wrap their weapon in cloth and wrap in plastic to keep it from the sand and the wind. I don't really know too much about the big gun maintenance, but they use COP too. And they have other lubricants, but that's their job. They constantly, every day you go on line and they're working, they work on those guns every day. And the vehicles, vehicles held up real well. HumV supply tons held up real well. We had a couple vehicles go down they would get them repaired and be back on the road. We had mechanics and wreckers with us. In our pos they were with us, but when the ground war started we had to jump, there'd just be a few people and then behind us would be the refuelers and their mechanics and then they would catch up with us. And a vehicle came down they would have to go up whatever the problem was and get that vehicle. They had a dangerous job.

For a while there we had a British retran site on our antenna hill and I didn't actually work with them, but I spoke with them. And I saw a lot of British. For a while there we had a British armored division attached to our task force and they were everywhere. They were very nice and enthusiastic.

I heard we had a lot of problems with the Saudis and stuff just because their thinking's not as aggressive as ours. I had some friends at Khafji and they had to be talked into doing things, but I thought it all went pretty good. We had a Kuwaiti officer with us and he was the translator and so we were able to communicate with anybody.

In training, the longest I was out in the field was like 22 days. We do a desert fox twice a year it's about 20-25 days.

The food was something, too. The MREs. If you make it right, the hot sauce was real popular. You'd use hot sauce. You'd heat them up by boiling water and use the squat stoves and we'd heat them up. But being in the Marine artillery you spend a lot of time in the fields so we knew how to cook up the concoctions.

When we first got there they were going to start us on malaria pills and then they cancelled it because the threat wasn't big enough and the Saudis provided water through their water plants and water never was a problem. Every once in a while they'd say hold back on the showers especially when the ground war started. No more showers, no more washing your clothes. We would wash our clothes by hand, but water never was a problem. The supply system was really good. We got two hot meals a day. We had breakfast and evening chow and MRE for lunch. Every once in a while if we'd be moving a lot it would take a couple days for it to catch up with us but I had no complaints about the food. I lost about 10 pounds. I weighed about a little over 170 when I left and I weighed myself about two days ago. I weighed about 163.

We had refuelers with us and headquarters battery had two refuelers and you always had to have your vehicle topped off. You're not allowed to run around with half full so if we were on exercise they'd had like what they called a jiffy mart was what they called it. A resupply point. You'd pull in and have a refueler set up and just go through and just keep going. But they sometimes had those LVSs set up.

We had two desert tans and one set of greens, we took over there. But it was just two sets. You don't want very much anyway. I had a pair of jungle boots, a pair of leather boots and in November, December a lot of us, our boots were starting to wear out. And I think it was in January, right before the ground war, they issued desert boots. And those are real comfortable. I really only saved one pair because the boots I had I had worn on the float and we had done so much time in the Philippines humping through the mountains and Thailand and stuff that they were already worn. The sand actually was real good to your feet.

I wasn't with the grunts' artillery. I'd truck it. We don't walk. I do a lot of walking 'cause everything's so spread out. Like if chow'd be in the center of the pos—that's our position, we just called it a pos—and antenna hill was about one klick away, about a thousand meters, about half a mile, you do a lot of walking.

I really wasn't worried much about it until we went through the second breach and we had some, we had the batallion—it came on the news, the Iraqis had two minefields set up. And having the grunts go through to secure the breach and the tanks come up. It's a big minefield. I think it was 300 feet, I'm not exactly sure of the measurements, but the Amtracks come up and they shoot that line charge over it and the line charge blew and then the tanks went through and then after it was secured then we went through, artillery. And we went through the second breach we set in a pause that night. We set up and we dug up holes and that night we pulled in and I saw some, they pulled in some dead Iraqi bodies, some bodies. And when I saw those that's when it hit me.

We left them there and the corpsmen tagged them and later that night, they had, you know, people had specific jobs and they came out and picked the bodies up and took care of them from there. We didn't have to . . . we didn't bury any bodies. They were all shipped out back to the rear.

We had several hundred EPWs surrender to the pos and, you know, they just walked up. One time, outside Kuwait airport, they just walked up carrying a white stick and they made everybody get on the perimeter and when they got to the pos they just put them on a truck and shipped them out. Our job wasn't to handle prisoners. Our job, 'cause we moved so fast we actually had, I was told one of the batteries had a lot surrender to them. They told them to wait. They said, "You sit right here. Don't move. Just sit down." There was several hundred of them. "Just sit down and don't move and somebody'll be by to pick you up."

The first thing you would, when they come to the pos, we'd try to get that Kuwaiti officer out there as soon as possible, but we were told to stop them and you secure them and you silence them. What you would do is you would put your rifle on them, secure them and put them on the deck face down and put their hands behind their head and you wouldn't go any further than that. You'd sit there and you'd wait until somebody came to help you because you're not supposed to search anybody by yourself.

You have a lot of security with these people 'cause supposing they could have been booby-trapped or they could say they're surrendering but they're not surrendering. But actually marines always travel together. You know, in the ground war there was no ground troops prisoners. Army had a lot of prisoners. But marines stay together. The recon outputs small units, but marines, we don't go driving off by ourselves.

That's the point it stops for us. That's the point it stops for me right there. Actually I'm just supposed to, my job if I ran into them, if I was on security, I was to get them on the ground and don't even touch them. We had a select security detail and they'd come up and they'd take it from there. And they would take them—just put them in a sort of a pos and we'd just wait for the grunts. And they would take care of it. But our job was not to do that.

A lot of them were lacking clothing. You know, their clothes were all torn and tattered and stuff. It's really strange 'cause a lot of them looked so much older than us. It was funny 'cause they had the big mustaches and here's this young marine, 18 years old, guarding an Iraqi looking like he was in his 30s. Looked like a boy guarding a man. You know, I'd say it was humiliating. Grown men surrendering, they thought they feared us a lot.

They thought we were baby killers. Actually they were happy once they got, once they were captured they would wave to you. You'd wave. They'd enjoy it. They had a good time. Once they were in our hands they were treated real well. A corpsman would look after them.

Far as we went was Kuwait City. We stopped right there. The Army supposedly was handling the Republican Guard. They're the ones that had the better equipment. We only had the M-60 tanks and they don't have the thermal sights and all. They had M-1s and the M-2s. A-1s and A-2s.

We set up outside Kuwait City. Not that many people went in. We set up outside of Kuwait City and when we did that we passed over control to the coalition forces, to the Saudis and the Kuwaitis. So a few people went in, but actually we didn't go in the city. Our artillery—we fire up on anywhere from 10 to 20 klicks away from our target so a lot of times we don't get to see it.

In the ground war I worked on antenna hill. My job was to get the antennas in the air, hook the com up, get ready to check with the units we were supposed to be talking to and then the FTC would take over, but yeah, that was one of my jobs when I worked in FTC was take a fire mission to the watch officer and he would decide what to do with it.

In headquarters battery and artillery, we'd get in trucks and go so the PT was actually kept up to yourself and we had some Saudis worked in our cement plant weld us some weights and we worked out with the weights and we used the old sand bags and stuff like that, but friends of mine that were with the grunts would have PT two, three times a week and they would have to go on humps. They had to stay in shape because they had to, a lot of them had to hump through the breaches. So their job was different.

One of our positions was set up on a hill and the gun line was in front of us and once we got the antennas up and dug in I could set there. I watched the first breach. It was real smoky and cloudy, but I could hear rounds going off, I could see tracers. It was really loud, but it was just very loud and noisy. I thought, when we were down there I thought, "I'm going to see some destruction!" But we went through the first couple breaches, there was a lot of Iraqis surrendering and a few Iraqi vehicles, but I was really surprised: I didn't see any Marine Corps vehicles down. And I was really happy 'cause they told us we'd have a lot of casualties.

They told us it was going to be comparable to World War II how the Germans, the trench line? But it wasn't.

They must have sat on their butts for six months 'cause I practiced breaches that were better done than theirs 'cause the mines were sitting on top of, you could actually see the mines on top of the sand. It was the wind, but they didn't go back and rebury them. It seemed like they laid the minefield. Actually the grunts they walked through the minefield. We had to blow holes so the vehicles could get through, but grunts could walk through, they could see the mines 'cause they were surface mines.

They had intel and the Iraqis do a good job of marking their minefields for us. Because there'd be a minefield and they'd run barbed wire in front and behind, so their own people wouldn't run into it. They could pull up, stop, throw the line charge over and then the engineers would go through and pick the mines up and then they would get some tanks through and then the engineers would go through and mark it, mark it with lanes so the vehicles could go through it.

When they were bombing, right before we went in, we moved real close to the border and I could feel the ground shake. It was the B-52s, we think they were our flights 'cause the ground really shook.

You wouldn't believe the mail we got. We got so much "Any Marine" mail—it was letters from children. We got a lot of care packages from people we didn't even know. I got, I was really surprised. Even friends of mine back home that I hadn't seen in a while, hadn't been in touch with, wrote me letters. I wrote my cousin—she's seven—from Atlanta and I wrote her whole class. A lot of people would write and a lot of times you'd get so down over there and you'd do the same thing every day people'd go what was it like over there you just wouldn't write. Sometimes we had to force ourselves to write.

We trained a lot. We'd spend a lot of time. We had a

lot of classes and things like that, but like Thanksgiving was a real down time 'cause we thought we'd be home at Thanksgiving, then everybody's hoping by Christmas, then everybody's hoping home by January, by February.

When I came back from Marsh Air Force Base at Twenty-Nine Palms, usually a two-hour drive, it took six hours. When we hit Rongo Valley the people were shaking our hands and giving us beer and food and girls giving us phone numbers. They really was. It was really nice. By the time we got to the base after, everybody's drunk.

In Saudi Arabia, there was no alcohol, no drugs. I think the only thing people came back with maybe they smoked coffee now.

A clean war.

ESTHER NEWMAN

Rank: Civilian
Duty: Moral Support
Hometown: Oceanside, California

Well, we been going down every Saturday to the rallies. We had three large ones. Our first one, downtown Oceanside in front of the Civic Center. We had about a thousand people show up for that one. The second, I think we had about 3,000, some of the media didn't give us that much credit, but that was how many people were there. We know, we were there. And on the third one, this last Saturday, we had like 5,000 people, screaming moms, marines' wives, moms, grandmas, children. It was absolutely the most exciting thing that ever happened to Oceanside and I've lived here for 35 years so I can testify that this was most wonderful thing.

I have some poems here, written by a friend. She lives by me and she's in a wheelchair. She was married to a Navy man for 27 years. And so she just, she writes poetry. She's written it throughout her life. This was most touching to me, the poem, the 18 poems that she's written so far and I imagine that as of this minute she's sitting at home right now. She couldn't come out here 'cause she's wheelchair bound, but I suppose she's probably writing poems right now.

The protesters? Not one of 'em showed up in Oceanside. But they did have protests every Saturday in Carlsbad and we were really proud of the fact that we didn't have any protesters. I tell you one interesting thing that did happen to me, though. See, I was the leader of the troops. I consider these people my troops. And I had my American flag, this is not the one 'cause I had a heavy duty handle here. And this is my American flag with a long yellow banner hanging from it. I was out there in the street and a police officer would come along and they'd say, "Esther, you gotta get your troops outta the street. You know, get 'em back!" And so they were, they were just neat and I'd keep telling 'em, "You guys are the best troops in the whole wide world." We screamed louder and harder and longer and we had our signs and our banners and everybody was there. But back to the protesters. One car did go by and they had an Iraqi flag inside the car and as they went by they held it up and waved it at me and gave me the finger. And that's the only protester I had and I just smiled back at him and waved at her just like every one of the rest of us.

When the war started, I was very worried. I prayed. I don't think I've ever prayed as hard as I prayed for this every day. I watched CNN every, I stayed up sometimes all night long. I watched CNN. I never went to sleep at all. And I was just draggy. I mean black, hollow eyes, just dragging around. We were all, everybody was so worried about them when it went to a ground war and boy, were we surprised because Stormin' Norman he went all the way and you know it was, it was great. He's my hero.

I was—This is funny. I hate to admit this and one of these days I'm going to write to President Bush. I did not vote for him. I am a Republican and I didn't vote for him because I thought he was a wimp. And this is terrible. I vote for the man, I don't vote for the party, I vote for the man. And right after he took office I wanted to write him and tell him, "I'm so sorry I didn't write, I didn't vote for you." I'm so ashamed because there's a saying, "Walk with"—one of the presidents, was it Theodore

Roosevelt—"Walk softly and carry a big stick." And I kept thinking about that. And I kept thinking about it. And I just, I am so ashamed I didn't vote for him. One of these days I am going to write him and I'm going to tell him this. And I hope either Colin Powell or Schwartzkopf is in there. My hero.

We rallied together. I have a T-shirt that on the back of and on the front it has Hussein as a camel laying under a tank and the guy is George Bush and he's in the tank. I wish you could see this shirt. He's in the tank holding this American flag and there's that camel with you know the little mustache—it's so cute. Then on the back I have the gal at the shop, I had her put "Our marines kick butt!" So this shirt and this T-shirt has been on, I mean, CNN was there. All our rallies. It's nothing to walk downtown Oceanside down the street. You can go down there right now and they'll all be there. You'll find everyone of these people, radio stations, newspaper reporters, will be downtown Oceanside looking for a story. But I would like to say something. KOCT interviewed me. This is our local Channel 37 television station. And I've never been interviewed before. They come up and they asked me, Brian Graham, he's a friend of mine, he said, "Esther, I want to interview you," and I says, "Oh, Brian," I said, "Go and interview the marine wives, you don't want to interview me." He says, "Yes, I want to interview you." And he says, "Why are you here?" And then I, oh! I was . . . .

And this was at the next to the last victory rally. And this was before that we knew that the war was gonna end. So this was, we were at our emotional peak. All these marine wives and all of this, mothers and aunts and uncles and everybody there. We were just, I cannot describe, other than you feeling it, the emotions that we felt and the pride that we felt in our country and our men at this time. And it just, he came to interview me and I was like a babbling idiot. He says, "Esther, why are you here?" And I just let it all spew out, you know, because we love America. We love each other. That's the main thing: 'cause we love each other. I just, you know, I was just talking, just babbling, so it was the most emotional moment, the highest emotion that a body could probably go to of being excited and thrilled and happy and so close to God.

I have to tell you, when the war first started I came out here to Camp Pendleton and I volunteered to go to Saudi, through the Red Cross. And so they sent me a thing out for Red Cross training in the mail and I got so involved in the, working in the rallies and all this here stuff and so involved in everything in the city that I never did get to the training so then I got to thinking, "Well, God is giving me, God made it so that I would be here to help the people here and you know to cheer and everything for our troops and I know one of the cameramen were going by for L.A., I think it was Channel 4, was walking by and I hollered over to the marines that were walking by and I told the guy that the marines were getting ready to ship out. I hollered at him, I says, "You guys fight the war over there, we'll fight the war here," and the reporter later come over and asked me you know if I really meant that. And I said that I meant it from the bottom of my heart.

What I meant, and I wanted to make sure that he knew what I meant, the protesters, and we felt like we were fighting the war here against the protesters. And we never had to meet 'em face to face. Now a lot of my friends went to Carlsbad and they did meet them face to face. But we were so busy with our positive stuff, going on here in Oceanside in our rallies here that we never got to Carlsbad to face off with 'em. But 45 of our people did go down there and they were on one side of the street and the protesters on the other side. It wasn't a big deal. It never made national news or anything. It wasn't that big a, it wasn't like there were thousands of people, you know, protesting and screaming and hollering. But there was a good probably hundred people there, 50 on one side of the street and 50 on the other side of the street. You know, I wish I could have gone. I really do. But I was too involved with our rallies here.

I didn't want to see them people anyway. Did you see the man on television that just got off the plane yesterday? And he said—oh, this was great—the little marine that got off the plane and he said, "Well, you know, how was it? How did you feel?" And he said, "Well," he said, "we saw all the, good to be home, and we saw all the wonderful things that the, the rallies that you did for us," and he said, "And to those protesters," he says, "we really don't care what you think." He gave a wink—like that. And I loved it. I love it! I would like to video tape that and keep it forever.

They never came to Oceanside. That's why. They didn't dare come to Oceanside because we were so positive and everything. I don't think one of them except for that, anybody dares set foot in Oceanside. They wouldn't, they would be ashamed to say it. We would all gang up on them, you know. Not physically, but you know, we would with our flags and waving and everything like that.

One last thing I'd like to say. Okay? I want you to know that I hugged at the rally, when we had this giant flag that they carried down Hill Street and it was spontaneous and they carried it down the, they gotta hang it on the building on Hill Street right now. They hung it on down. And thousands of us just fell out into the street behind the flags. Before that happened whenever the VFW—these are the guys from Pearl Harbor. There were some Pearl Harbor survivors. And they all had their hats and their badges and their ribbons and everything on, Pearl Harbor survivors. So I was a little girl during the second World War and I went up and hugged every single one of 'em. And it was really neat. One guy said, "Can I have an extra squeeze?" I thought that was cute.

This thing that's coming up on April the 27th is going to be the biggest thing they ever had. The marines are going to run their troops down Hill Street. The marines are going to run their band down there. They're going to run their equipment, all their troops. They're going to run their, our kids, the high school bands are going down there. They going to have parachutists from the airplanes and helicopters and going to drop onto the beach. We're going to have fireworks. With a little bit of luck we're going to have Tom Cruise and my hero, my 'nother hero, Gerald McRaney, who was in the Marine Corps out here at Camp Pendleton. They're getting 'em now. Bob Hope wanted to do it, but he had a previous engagement. Barbara Mandrell had a previous engagement. We're going to wind up with a whole bunch of stars and hundreds of thousands of people. The parade's going to go from Oceanside to Carlsbad, it's going to be so long. It's going to be the most incredible thing that's ever happened.

The Chamber of Commerce is doing that. I'm just going to be one of the ones that's going to be there decorating and doing anything that needs to be done. I will be there to do it. I've done it for 35 years. I've decorated that stadium so many times! When the King of Samoa came over I got to decorate it.

CHRISTOPHER T. SANFORD

Rank: Sergeant
Service: Army
Duty: Infantry
Hometown: Boston, Massachusetts

My wife had a baby girl on the 23rd of January. Her name's Courtney Marie. I got in Saudi Arabia on the 8th of August, out of Fort Bragg, North Carolina.

It was . . . it was dirty, mainly, you know. It wasn't—it didn't seem like it was too much to be worried about. There was a lot of outgoing artillery, but not so much any incoming where we were at. We weren't that close to the actual artillery pieces. They were well behind us.

I didn't shower for about 35 days. *(Laughs.)* Oh, we had — you know, shave out of a canteen cup. But you know, there was no problem about getting resupplied with water or anything like that. It was hot—120, 125 degrees. When we first moved north, it got really cold. But it dropped in the thirties, below freezing. We woke up the first night we moved north, we woke up and everything I had was covered with frost. That's the first time I've seen frost. *(Laughs.)*

Everything, everything came through, you know, as far as stuff to keep us warm and keep us fed. You know, little gadgets and everything we wanted, they took more time.

We did a lot of directing for the EPWs. We had a Kuwaiti guy attached to my team, and he did a lot of interviewing with them, interrogating. We were attached to the French. And that was kind of cool. They—I don't think they did the job they should have done, but . . .

I think it was just their command which really messed up. The guys were trained, they knew—they were trained more specific than we are, I think. The tankers I met, they had one job, one gun or one driver. And the driver didn't know anything about doing the gunner's job or anything like that.

They weren't cross-trained. But they knew their stuff. I watched a couple of T-54's blow up. The only artillery I saw—they had big guns, but the only time I saw any of it was after it had been destroyed. Because the Air Force did a hell of a job. We came up on a bunker that had a 2.5 millimeter rocket, sticking up through the top of the bunker, that hadn't exploded. You know, deadly accurate. One building they hit, they dropped the bomb through the chimney and one through a window. From the outside of the building, it looked like just the window had been knocked out. From the inside there was nothing.

And the Iraqis had no will to fight. It was—there was like a big variance. Some of them looked like they were eating well and everything. Some of them looked like they were eating real well. *(Laughs.)* But then there were other guys that didn't have boots, didn't have anything. Well, socks. There were a lot of people throwing everything they had away, just trying to totally separate themselves from being in the military. You know, they killed one of the commanders because the dude didn't want to surrender.

We were up in—we had just crossed the border into Iraq, we were just sitting there, it was at night, and we were waiting, we were waiting to move out in the morning. And all of a sudden this MRLS, you know, 250 meters away starts firing. And nobody knew it was—none of us knew it was there. And they just started firing. It scared the hell out of everybody. It was our stuff.

And we were just sitting in our vehicles ready to roll. It was weird, you know, we trained so much, and digging in and everything. But when we actually came across, there wasn't time, you know. We'd stop, when we'd stop, we stop for like three hours, but we'd be gone, we'd move again.

There was nobody to stop us. The first day we had actual contact with the enemy, I saw these guys, about four guys came out of this one bunker, and they had a huge, huge white flag. Two guys were waving it, three by six. It was huge. That looked like it was, like it was out of a sheet or something. But they had been firing off their flares to get the parachutes off of them. Just to have something white.

These guys were like . . . "We had fires going for two days, you know, why didn't you come?" The Iraqis had fires going to let us know where they were.

TAMARA L. LINK

Rank: Captain
Service: Air Force
Duty: Nurse
Hometown: Unknown

I'm an air evac nurse. I was down there for six months. I got there September 7th. I originally set up in one location.

There were a lot of guard and reserve air evac folks down there which was an experience in itself trying to learn to deal with a lot of them because—a lot of them were inexperienced. A lot of them were much more experienced than myself, but a lot of them had never flown live air evac missions with real patients before so there was a lot of training involved.

I fly, I'm tri-qualified: I fly C-9s as a flight nurse, obviously, C-141s and C-130s. Our primary job down there was flying C-141s, flying from in the theater to somewhere in Europe to drop off the patients. They were long missions. Those were considered the strategic air evac missions. Initially, it was, it was flying out a lot of people that shouldn't have been there in the first place: people with history of cardiac problems, people with casts on their arms already that shouldn't have ever been deployed down there. People that obviously couldn't function in that environment. But I think because they deployed them so rapidly they just took everybody so a lot of people had asthma that they couldn't tolerate the dust and the sandstorms and all that stuff. Some people had diabetes and medical problems that really they couldn't really function.

I'm active duty stationed in Germany. Initially, we did not have very many casualties. It was mostly accidents, people that would break their feet or break their arms, things like that. And, actually, we didn't have that many casualties in this war. Thank God! You know, it was like we were, we were warming up for the Super Bowl and we never got to play. We were ready to move 2,000 casualties a day and we never did so it was, you know, and in an ironic way it was a little disappointing that we didn't get to live up to that professional challenge that we were all geared up for, but yet every single one of us was thanking God every day for the fact that we didn't have all those people injured.

I did move a couple of people that had injuries, some helicopter pilots that had crashed, that were pretty seriously injured, a couple of guys that were in the Dhahran SCUD attack that had lost their legs and things like that. And it's really sad to see that. You see one of those guys and you just look and think, "This could have been a whole lot more than this guy," and you have a lot of empathy for that guy right there because you know it's changed his life.

The patients came in on C-130 missions. We, I didn't get to fly a C-130 mission, I flew a training mission, but they would fly up into the front lines and pick up the patients on the C-130 and bring them back. Those are the tactical missions and they're fast and furious and basically get the people on, throw them on the plane and get out. Because you never know when hostile fire's going to hit. You never know when something's going to happen or the base is going to be overrun that's supposedly secured. After they get them from there, they bring them back to the strat hub is what they call and they'll go into one of the hospitals, one of the air transportable hospitals or a . . .

Some of them are just tents. Actually the Air Force has nicer hospitals than the Army does. The Air Force has temper tents which are a lot more comfortable. They're air-conditioned, and they just seem more comfortable.

Where I was the sky was kind of darkened a little bit. I mean you couldn't actually see a big oil cloud. The sky was dark, it looked kind of eerie in the day sometimes. The sun would be shining through and you'd blink at the end of the day and you'd be wondering if it was the sun or the moon. But I think, we all think that it was the oil cloud and the weather got really strange. It got sort of rainy a lot and it got extremely windy which was unusual for this time of the year. It really just got bad.

The patients were pretty much stabilized by the time we got them. They took them, there's various, the medical system's set up so there's a lot of Army hospitals around, a lot of Air Force hospitals. They took the patients initially to those facilities and treated them and then once they were stable enough to tolerate an eight to ten hour flight then we got them. Now some of them were still pretty seriously injured.

I flew the POW mission. I was one of the flight nurses. On TV they looked pretty beat up. Some of the guys, their faces. I flew the second air evac mission. We picked them up in Riyadh and took them out to the Mercy which is a Navy hospital ship, obviously. And they looked really good. They were ecstatic. They were so happy. We were told that they might be weak and they wanted us to escort each ambulatory patient, walk right beside them in case they were weak and needed to hold on to us. They didn't want to have anything to do with us! They were so excited to get off that plane.

I talked to some of them that said they weren't really beat up too bad. I took care of the Army flight surgeon a lot, the lady with the two broken arms. Rhonda. Cohen? She said the worst thing that happened to her was her arms were broken and the Iraqis changed their locations a lot.

They were set. I'm not sure who set it to be quite honest, but she had some pretty poor looking casts on her arms that weren't really very good casts, but at least it was holding her arms a little bit and they were really sore. I mean you had to handle her very gently because she was really sore. But she said the Iraqis had been, had dragged her around a little bit, I mean with her broken arms before they were set. It was really painful for her.

I talked to, I'm going to try to remember his name, Strom—was that the guy? He was an A-10 pilot and they thought he was dead. And his roommate—they had escorts for all of the POWs, they had escorts from their squadron to meet them. And they also had medical escorts. And this guy, they said, "We had written him off. We thought he was dead." And all of a sudden they find out that he's alive after all which was really interesting.

Some of them were, some of them were right there, I think it was Colonel Eberly that had ejected and he landed and was right on the radio and they were right there like a couple hundred yards from him and on the radio they, he was saying, "They're coming for me." You know, and he said, "I have to go off the radio now. They're coming for me." That's not a direct quote but it was something along that line.

They had spent time in various POW camps throughout Iraq. They moved them around quite frequently and eventually they ended up in Baghdad. They were mostly in solitary confinement. I don't think it was the little box.

Basically, they didn't really describe the physical layout but they were kept apart from the other POWs so they didn't have any access to them. Although they said when the soldiers would go away they could talk to each other a little bit through the walls.

I think they were able to communicate fairly well. At one point they took them to a camp that was pitch black. It was just really dark and they really couldn't see anything. I don't think, I don't know if they blindfolded them or not but they said that was pretty scary.

They didn't say anything about torture. They looked good. They were very thin. They had all lost like 25 or 30 pounds. They said they ate about two pieces of pita bread a day and something that they all called blood soup, every single one of them, they were like "Oh, yeah, we had our blood soup." And they said if you picture blood making a soup out of blood this is what it looked like. They said it was a thin, the one guy said, "No. I would call it thin tomato broth with beef grease." And, you know, that was about all they had was this greasy tomato soup and a couple pieces of pita bread. And every once in a while they had rice. So they had all lost a lot of weight, especially the ones who had been captured the longest.

I do know they were in Baghdad and when the, I think when the allies were bombing Baghdad some of the POWs camps were affected by it. They were strong. They were very strong. I was surprised how strong they were. They all seemed very mentally stable. But I think with any kind of trauma like that they're in a hyperalert state for so long you never know if you're going to be killed, you never know what's going to happen to you and you get used to functioning on a level ten, you know, and I think when they go back to the real world, quote unquote, they're going to have, they may have a hard time adjusting right away. As anybody would, I think coming back from a situation like that. I think they might have, they're going to have some counseling, I'm sure through their branches of service just to help them make sure that they're dealing with it okay.

I talked to an F-15 pilot that had been up and he said that it was really exciting. They didn't quite know what to expect but it was—finally, you know, finally they got to do their jobs, you know, finally they're going in and they were flying close air support for some of the other, I can't remember what they were flying close air support—their mission wasn't actually, it was more just protecting the planes that they were flying with and, us, actually the one guy that I talked to who's an F-15 pilot out of Langley said that after a while it got pretty routine. You know, even flying into Iraq it got pretty routine after a while. He said they always had the little triple A firing at them and that kind of their adrenaline going so that they could fly the mission. 'Cause they'd go there and they'd CAP, combat air patrol, and he said that would get kind of boring after a while. But their missions were real long, too.

They went from the Mercy. They were all taken to the Mercy and eventually they all went back to Andrews Air Force Base. There's three different hospitals there, I think that they went to. It was really interesting. We also carried enemy prisoners of war which was interesting, too.

I'm not sure where they took them but according to the Geneva convention we treat patients. We don't care if they're enemy, we don't care if they're American. If they're hurt, we treat them. They looked, a lot of them looked very, very thin. A lot of them—I talked to one of the nurses that flew a mission and she said a lot of them had like blown off arms and blown off legs and I don't know who did it. I don't think it was the Americans, I think it was the Iraqis, but they basically put them in baggies and sent them along with patients, I guess, in hopes of reattaching the limb. And the patients were carrying them.

I didn't fly any of those missions, but I talked to a lot of people who did and they said that you don't know what to expect. You think you're going to go in and you're going to be mad at these people 'cause we're at war with them. But she said once you looked at them, they're just normal people and your compassion just flowed for them 'cause they were really hurt some of them and they love the United States. A lot of them would do a thumbs up and they'd say "George Bush, yaay!" you know? They really liked, they liked the Americans and they were really excited to get out of there, I think.

As a matter of fact, a lot of them didn't have any shoes at all. They were in their bare feet and they would pick them up and one of the nurses that I was talking to had to walk them across this compound and there were stones, you know, like gravel, and she felt so bad because none of these guys had shoes on but there was nothing they could do so she sort of put an arm around them and took them by the arm and kind of helped them walk across this gravel. But she couldn't believe they didn't have shoes on, some of them. Some of them they said looked pretty good. They were pretty healthy guys and, you know, they looked fairly healthy but a lot of them were really sick and malnourished and obviously excited to be out of the war and out of Saddam's regime.

I heard there was a lot of Iraqi resistance going on and I heard that Saddam has threatened to kill the families of soldiers if the soldiers deserted and things like that. And I guess their way of getting out of it was to surrender, you know, especially when they came up upon the Americans who were kicking their butts.

My mother had put my picture in the paper under Operation Support of Soldiers and I must have received 150 letters from people, half of them I didn't know, you know, that were like, "We love you! We're praying for you. God bless you! I hope it's over soon." And it was just incredible that the support that we got from the States. It really made a big difference for us.

LAWRENCE E. MCKAY

Rank: Sergeant
Service: Army
Duty: Intelligence
Hometown: Charleston, South Carolina

I'm 30 years old. I turned 30 in the desert. It was interesting. What I am is I'm 66 Military Intelligence and my job mainly is an analyst. I analyze whatever kind of intelligence we receive and write reports on it and try and figure out what the enemy's doing and what our best avenue is.

We have units that went out and different elements that would intercept different things. Fortunately we were able to tie everything in through the communications link—that normally we didn't have before—that tied in all the corps. We had AM communications which helped a lot. And as far as the units, there really wasn't a hell of a lot that were out there, which was kind of surprising. And a lot of times we thought we were just missing things. And it turned out that they had just pulled back so far that we weren't getting anything on the front lines and in that area.

In fact, we picked up seven POWs that were supposed to go out to the Republican Guards that were going out as replacements because they had been losing so many people from our bombing raids. And they said for two weeks they had been wandering the desert because they weren't going to report to the unit because they didn't want to die. And they weren't really bothered by any of the other units that they ran into because they figured that they were an elite squad because they were outfitted with the Republican Guard uniforms and everything.

The Republican Guard wore—I don't know if I can say this right—a tongwin and the Republican Guard had a red triangle or actually crimson triangle patches but they were made out of velvet-type material that most of them cut out themselves. They varied from a light red, almost an orange, to crimson. And that was the main way that you could tell. On their helmets they would have either a red triangle or a circle. They were outfitted with new boots and new uniforms and protective masks and all of that kind of thing.

The Republican Guard was Saddam's elite attack force. That is what he used mainly for his major assaults into Iran and that's what he used mainly to go down in Kuwait and take everything and secure. And once he secured it, then he brought in his reserve forces which he had back in Baghdad and that area from the outskirt areas. And they came in and they secured the line and the Republican Guard pulled back as a defensive area. In case we ever went across it, they were supposed to come and put down an engagement.

They weren't getting any food. We talked with some POWs who said that they were getting a piece of bread—in other words, half a piece of bread in the morning and half a piece of bread at dinner—and a bowlful of rice for lunch. And that's what they were eating down on the front lines.

Now the Republican Guard was still getting supply lines from Baghdad. When we went in there, there was lots of rice that was left over. There were a lot of dates and fruit that the Republican Guard was getting that the front line units weren't.

The bunkers—a lot, especially out near the northern

part of Iraq—were corrugated steel pipes that they had just put under ground. And they made a small tunnel network and most of it was dirt bunkers. They really weren't that well reinforced. If any kind of reinforcement, they used a cinder block. We had heard in the past that they were cement-reinforced, three-foot-wide walls. Well, most of the stuff that we ran into, the way that we went up there, was not that.

We were never targeted for any SCUD attacks. The 7 Corps only received one and they don't even know if that was by accident. Most of the SCUD attacks were directed directly either at Saudi cities or at Israel.

Most of the POWs that I saw were from the Republican Guard and most of them were still so well-clothed. A lot of the other units that swept wider on either side of us were picking up the reserve units. We were mainly targeted towards the Republican Guard.

The main thing that will stand out the rest of my life is that, going through almost the whole war, we just shot straight up into Iraq with hardly any kind of resistance whatsoever. It was mainly a surrender-type thing and the only real engagements were as they were pulling out their forces to go up to Baghdad. It's kind of amazing that you would go into a country that we were almost invading—well, we were invading, not almost. We were invading their country and they weren't even really fighting for it. And that's something that's hard for us to contemplate. But also when you look at their country, it is really a desert wasteland and all of the 600 kilometers that we covered going up was almost deserted except for a few Bedouins, Arab sheep herders. They herd sheep and they herd camels. And they have their families out there. And we waved to them as we were going up there and they would wave back.

One of the big fears was that we would come across Bedouins that would have hostile feelings against us and that that would be where we would get our casualties—not from the real units but from unknown sources. And the thing was that we never really engaged any real defensive forces. They didn't dig in. The thing was, because of the air superiority, that these units had not air attack themselves or air cover. And when our planes went over, the only defense that they had was to run. And in fact, one thing that some of the POWs said also is that for the last half of the war, from about two weeks into the air battle, they would take their tanks and park them up on the embankments so that they were targets and would then go down into a valley and dig a bunker. And that's where they would spend the nights. They would park the tanks up so that they would be a target and the units would stay down so that their tanks would be destroyed.

Most of the mine fields were haphazard, fairly easy to detect. We did bombing raids on mine fields. It's a set-up bomb, a fuel bomb, that explodes. The concussion gives 400 lbs. of ground pressure and that's enough to explode any land mines. And that would destroy a whole mine field. We'd locate them through intelligence and through aerial reconnaissance.

Because of the time period with the air superiority, we could have the reconnaissance planes and the helicopters go deeper into the lines. The ADA were very sporadic; the Anti-Air was very sporadic and they didn't have the sophistication to move it around. So most of it was located around their airfields in that area, areas that they wanted to protect so it was real easy to skirt around with.

There was one officer, their officer POW, who's exact quote was, "Hussein is an asshole" And that was about all he said and the same with the seven POWs that we picked up. They were not going to go to the Guard. One officer that we interviewed was kind of interesting. He said that it would cost so much to take our equipment back, he wondered why we just didn't leave it there for them and let them use it, which is something that I guess kind of gives you insight as to how loyal they really were to Hussein. There were very few, even the Republican Guards anymore, that are loyal to him.

I believe a backlash is already happening now with the Shiites because the majority of the population is Shiite. And even the forces that he had against us were mainly Shiite. And the Kurds, with what he had done to them years ago... His reign of power is definitely coming to an end.

What we did is we took a westerly approach; we came from the west, Saudi Arabia, went up through Iraq and went to the northern part of Kuwait. And we didn't actually go into Kuwait itself because what we were mainly interested in were the Republican Guards that were based outside of Kuwait and that were supposed to be used as reserves. You wonder if they just opened up avenues for us to drive through. And that was one thing that we had contemplated even before all of this happened. We saw pockets that we thought were going to be fire pockets that he was going to try and sucker us into and because we did not see activity in certain areas. But it was mainly because there was no activity.

General Schwarzkopf did a great job at organizing the Navy, the Marines and the Air Force, something that we've never done before, which was blatantly obvious when we tried to go and rescue the hostages before. And it was amazing that we even got, with the Arab countries, that there was such camaraderie with the coalition forces.

We had Kuwaitis serving with us as linguistic support and they came in. They were real interesting people to have around because it gives you an insight more into this area and you get to understand what the people feel in this area. Kuwait is an advanced city compared to Iraq and even to Saudi Arabia as far as accommodations that they have and everything. And one thing that one of the Kuwaitis said in an address was that this was a terrible thing to happen but that he was glad that our histories were now meshed as countries and that he sees a lot of good coming out of this in the future.

We worked with Kuwaitis, as far as linguists and that kind of stuff. We really did not work with the Saudis that much, the Saudis and the Syrians. But as far as using the Kuwaitis as linguists, it helped us out immensely because, like I said, not only did it give us a linguistic support but it also gives you cultural understanding. And you know, it's amazing, their ideas like, with women and that kind of stuff. We had women linguists and you could tell that this was not really accepted by them. And it's still not accepted by their government. And that's what's going to be so hard with them trying to go into a democracy—trying to get them to recognize women.

Most of our information went back to Corps; what we would get we would send back. And except for the actual forward observers—also, again, coming from POWs—they were ordered not to communicate on the radios for a four-month period. The Iraqi soldiers. In fact, they confiscated some of their radios just to cut down on the radio traffic so that there wouldn't be that much intelligence gleaned off of what they had.

Where we were is, we were right up on the Saudi-Iraqi border, just about. That night we saw a few B-52s going over but mainly where we were was an avenue of approach where they had done all of their practice bombing raids earlier. And instead of really using that, I believe they used different avenues of approach because it was a run that they went up to the main supply drops that we were going to use and then they would veer back—our planes would. This was before the actual bombing. And then on the night of the actual bombing, we saw a few flying over but most of it was targeted more towards Kuwait.

Everyone was glad that something was happening. We figured that we'd be going in, at the very most, at two weeks. We didn't expect it to hold off for a full month. Everyone was really glad that it was happening, that something had started, because we'd been in-country for four and a half months at that time. Once we had Christmas —everyone figured that maybe we were going to wait until Christmas. We knew that, at the very most, we should wait until maybe the first of the new year because we knew that the Saudis wanted us out of here by Dahaj, by the beginning of Dahaj.

Dahaj starts, I believe, on March 17. That's where all of the Moslems make a pilgrimage to Mecca—or it's part of their religious rites. They're required to make a pilgrimage to Mecca and to Medina. And they wanted the Saudi border opened up.

SALLEY O. MORRIS

Rank: Corporal
Service: Marine Corps
Duty: Ordinance
Hometown: Kaneohe, Hawaii

Part of my mission over there was to build ordnance for all the squadrons who supported—we had two AC squadrons, four F/A 18s, which included the Deltas, the AD and then we had a Q2 out there.

When we get in, all the necessary supplies and equipment that come in, you have the hard bodies—it depends on what type of mission they're going at, what kind of target they're going at. You decide what kind of fuse you want to put in, and what kind of . . . how you're going to arm them and how they're going to fly away.

We got to load bombs on the airplanes. When the squadrons were short and we were down on line. Mostly we do . . . and transport them down the line. We had a day crew and a night crew and we in the overlap. We were working anywhere from 12 to 16 hours a day. And that was non-stop. And that included all the weapons . . . when I was told I was going to be leaving. I got there on the 13th of December.

I'm divorced. And I have a daughter at home—a two-year-old. My mother and father took care of her.

You know how it gets—your horror will take you back and all of a sudden, you'd be like . . . even now, when I hear the fire alarm go out the other day we all jumped and we were looking around and then we started laughing because we realized it was kind of funny, but we didn't put our MOPP gear on unless it was by the direction of one of the commanding officers to wear it.

We had Patriot missiles right on the base. We went out to see what they could find and what they couldn't. We were standing around talking and all of a sudden we saw this flash of light and it landed on—we just kind of stood there and we were like, "Is that what I think it is?" And then it was like this small explosion—you could see it burning right off the base. And we were just like . . . then they called it up to the radio and they said "Put your gas masks on."

By then I was just pissed. It's too goddamned late. I said the goddamned thing is . . . we were just kind of joking around, laughing and then he comes down to us and tells us the CO wants us to go. . .by then the alarm had already sounded. By then the thing had already been on the ground for about three or four minutes. It was kind of funny. So I stood there laughing.

When the Patriots launch off, it's just a light. The first time we saw it, it went right up over the flat line. The only thing that got to us was that safety was first but that wasn't—I mean we tried to do as much as can, because. . .they had to get out and get a mission out there because if it was up to them—they relied on us because if we didn't get it to them they can't get out there and then we'd have troops out there dying. . .we were pretty calm even when they said, "We need 300 bombs on line now, they've got to be flown out at such and such time, I don't care how you get them out, just get them out."

And we'd be out there, just throwing things together. We did as much safety precautions as possible but you know, we had our share of accidents out there. Just like everybody else. No one got hurt or killed or anything, but I'm talking like we'd drop things, run over things, and . . . but if I had it to do all over again, I'd go back out there.

SHUNJIE G. DURHAM

Rank: Airman First Class
Service: Air Force
Duty: Supply
Home State: South Carolina

I'm 20 years old. Actually, my experience over there in Saudi Arabia, it was very dull for us and made us feel very tied in—being that I am a female and the customs, being very strict, they don't care too much for women and any time we had to go anywhere we had to be escorted or when we'd go downtown or anything like that, we had to wear like robes, and we had to wear the cape over our heads. The worst thing of all was that we couldn't drive at all.

We had to purchase the robes ourselves and sometimes it was hard. A lot of times you know, with us being so Americanized, we would wear shorts, if we wanted to, underneath the robes but we had to have on the robe. In Saudi Arabia you're not allowed to let parts of your body show. And in the States you can wear jeans or T-shirts or whatever, but in Saudi Arabia they don't like to see you in jeans and they like for you to cover up your arms and everything like that.

I got to Saudi Arabia in August so I went down to the town there quite a few times. I was in supply. I did everything that the guys did. I drove a forklift, pooled property, put up property, ran computers, you know, all around . . . on the base.

CURT A. JOHNSON

Rank: Lance Corporal
Service: Marine Corps
Duty: Light Armor
Hometown: Brownsburg, Indiana

Well, first we're there, we trained a lot, setting out in the desert and then, the closer to the day that we were supposed to be going in in the land and everything, we started moving up reconning the area to get better positions and stuff in case they would start attacking us, we'd have places to fall back on.

I was a driver, a TOW driver. It's a, it's a 25, it's a variant. A TOW vehicle is mounted, a TOW is mounted on a 25. It's kind of hard to explain. It's a missile, a TOW missile, that's anti-tank. There's four people on the vehicle. There is a driver, a VC—a vehicle comander—a TOW gunner, and an A gunner.

I got over there September 8th. It was very hot and the flies there were just terrible, terrible. They'd try to fly in your mouth and it just, it was terrible. Hot, I'd say maybe 110, 115. We weren't really sure because we were in a, at first we were in like a hangar-type barn and there was no air going through there and it was very hot there. Then we moved out to the desert when our vehicles got there. We started doing maneuvers and stuff and the flies, you know, you'd move from one position to the other and there'd be dead camels there and the flies just, it was terrible.

There was like camie nets and it was just like a, just a net with camouflage on it and you'd live in that and then, we lived in that for maybe two months when we got there and then they decided that they didn't want the nets there. They wanted us to be ready to go at a second's notice. And we started just living on the ground. Just gave our cots up, everything. And you just slept on the, in your sleeping bag on the floor.

And there were snakes, too. They really didn't get inside your sleeping bag, they just crawled up next to you to keep warm and you'd lift up your sleeping bag or your poncho that you had the sleeping bag on and there might have been, you know, some scorpions.

Communications were kind of slow. It was like we'd ask our captain, "What's going on, what's going on?" He would, he would tell us what's going on and then that was it. That's the only word we'd really had. It wasn't very much.

I didn't even know it started that night. Because there was a guy on a, he was a vehicle watch and in the distance he saw just glowing things and then we'd put the NVGs on, which is our night vision goggles, and when we did that we could, we could see the war. Then. And hear it. But we weren't really sure. It was just, we'd hear noises, you know.

We were attached to the 25s. The 25 millimeter gun, the gun, the LAV 25s. And it was usually eight of them. Eight of them and eight of us. And we would go out with them and we'd be security for them. They would take out anything smaller than a tank, like a BMP. That is a, it's a tank variant, but it's small, where their rounds can pierce it and just, you know, like if they came up to a T-62 or anything like that caliber we'd move up, take it out and then they would keep on going and we'd go with them.

I was, I was real scared. I didn't know, I was confused, at first we were confused and then when we realized, you now, they're firing at us, then we started maneuvering.

We have thermal night sights and they don't have any thermal capability, the Iraqis. So we saw them coming long before, they didn't even know we were there and then when we started lighting them up that's when they started firing at us, but they really didn't know where we were because they couldn't see us. And we can see, you know, we can see pretty far out with those because we're picking up thermal heat images. Where we moved up, like at the berm—we stayed at the berm for maybe about a week, maybe two weeks before we went in.

The border ends right there. And we moved up there and we had surveyed, just surveillance, mainly, to make sure, you know, see the enemy, see where they're going and stuff.

This was Kuwait. We were up there with Shepherd. And what Shepherd did when they went through. Ripper went through first. It made the breach. And then Shepherd came through and put a screen line up so that night, 'cause I guess they thought there was going to be a real big battle when they went through and everything.

We put a screen line up so they could refuel and everything and then after that we just detached and they did their job and we did our job. We launched our missiles at them and the 25s.

When the TOW goes off, you can't feel anything because it's tube-launched and there's, it's just a rocket and all, it's like if you've ever shot a bottle rocket or something or those, those flare-shooting-up-things, it's just like that. Just whoosh and then it's gone.

You can see them through the NVGs, all you see is when it comes out, the TOW, it'll drop a little bit and then you'll see its boosters kick in and they'll start going and then the gyros will start kicking and then that's when the missile takes off, and it's armed. And there's a probe that comes out about like 36 inches probably and what that does is, that's the, the armor piercing system and that puts the hole in the tank and then it shoves all the explosives inside the tank and then it blows the whole tank up.

We've got two TOWs in the system at all times and then we got 14 inside the vehicle. If we use all the ordnance and need more, there's the combat train and the FARP teams will bring it up to you. Every day we'd get fuel and water. The TOW vehicle can probably go about 300, maybe 400 miles.

You know, when I'm driving, you know, going by all these blown up vehicles I'm going "You know, this could be us!" You know, 'cause all you can see out is the vision blocks and there's three of them. And that's all I've got to look out of and they're about an inch and a half by six inches. And they got three of them and then the VC, he's the only one that can really see anything 'cause he's out standing up. That's the vehicle commander.

He can only, he'd be the only one that could see anything and he's telling you where to go plus he's looking around making sure there's nobody jumping up with RPG's or, you know, any kind of thing that can destroy you. And it was pretty scary going through there and, you know, you'd see like tracers shoot in from the vehicle and you'd see it coming at you and it was pretty scary.

The first time we saw them, okay, the first, the first engagement we had, they were in like a column going south. They were going somewhere and then we engaged them and then they just broke up and air got called in and that night we destroyed like 25 tanks and so many other types of vehicles. I went through a lot of tanks.

They were badly maintained. You could tell they were by just going inside of them, looking at the components. They weren't taken care of, you know. The ones that need oil they weren't oiled. It was pretty bad. They were rusty. Rusty around the engine where you could pick up to look into the engine it was rusty.

Once we went in, I really didn't sleep. If I did sleep, it'd been in the driver's compartment, you know, just setting there and waiting to go because you didn't know when you were going to leave and when you're not, you know. You had two seconds. You didn't know.

We'd leapfrog, bounding. And we didn't launch all of our missiles at once. It wasn't like that. Once we hit them, and because they're used to fighting at like 1,000 to 500 meters and we're taking them out like 3,000 and plus meters so they didn't have a chance to even come near us. There was no aggression towards us. They were very scared and it would be like one, one would come out and give himself up and then they'd just all start coming. All of them.

It wasn't our job to—our headquarters would take all the prisoners in. They'd just, they'd walk up to us, you know, and we'd flag them, go behind us, and we'd just drive right by them. We kept them far enough away from us where, you know, and the coax was on them, you know, we have like a M-60 and that was on them at all times when we'd go by them in case something would happen.

I honestly don't want to remember any of it, except maybe the better times we had over there. Like before we went in we had time to play football and get in games of football and stuff like that. When we were over there, we lost four people from our section . . . friends. They were hit by a tank. It blew up their vehicle. That'd probably be the memories I'd keep—playing football and talking and messing around with those guys.

RICHARD DOOLEY

Rank: Civilian
Duty: Computer Intelligence Expert
Hometown: Arlington, Virginia

I'm from Arlington, Virginia. Born and raised there and fortunately I work just outside of there in Vienna, Virginia. The reasons that I went to Desert Storm were twofold. Basically, my company developed computer systems that were being used by the US Air Force in theater to do intelligence processing and you've heard it from others, too. Reasons that I went over there was to support the hardware aspect of the operation. We had numerous systems at various locations throughout the entire theater there and for the most part they were all running and in pretty good shape. Some of the platforms that we had working over there were based on computers that were running at a much slower processing speed than some of the other systems that were in theater so my main job to go there was to upgrade those systems to work at a higher rate of speed and thus provide a lot more capability of early warning and intelligence processing for these guys.

The thing is that when I found out that the war had started I was very surprised but at the same time—I was coming back from the airport in Washington, D.C., to my house and the cab driver had it on the radio and I had feelings that I just kind of wanted to go there. And I think that was based on the fact that you know the systems that I work on we've had out in the field in various different formats for a few years and I've kind of grown up with them.

And it's a chance to see them really, well, we always

believed that they were good systems and that they provided something that was extremely valuable to the customer and this was a chance to really be there and see it doing its job. I mean, we already knew that it was doing its job because we had a unit back in our own home office and it was doing everything it was supposed to do. And the opportunity for me to be able to be there and see that happening in a real life situation was an opportunity that I couldn't really pass up, but that was something that was hard to sell to my wife and family, you know.

I was in the Navy for six years and never saw any combat duty or anything like that, it was all peacetime stuff, but you know my wife and family were really upset, they were like "Why the hell are you going there?" And they thought it was some sort of a macho trip, you know, just "I want to be in the war," but it really wasn't that at all. It was just an opportunity to help support a system that I really believe helped save a lot of lives over there.

Can't really tell you a whole lot about what it does, but I think that most of the people that know about our system would agree from the Air Force side of the house that if they didn't have the data that our system provided things might have been a lot different there. And that was just a great opportunity to be there. The other thing that really struck me as being a very unique and rewarding experience was once I finally got to the site in Riyadh and was working in the compound it was working in an environment that was pretty severe in the fact that it was a place where you wouldn't expect to be running computer systems in a very high degree.

And everybody's teamwork was phenomenal there. I've done a lot of work on shipboard applications and this was one hundred times more severe than any of those. The heat, the dust, the lack of good power, the lack of basic necessities like electrical outlets, extension cords, things like that. But everybody chipped in and worked together to get everything working and nobody seemed to really mind that much that they were working in that kind of an environment. And it was the Navy, it was the Air Force, it was the Army and it was the contractors all alike, working hand in hand and it was very impressive.

As a matter of fact I talked to my wife tonight and I told her that I had an opportunity to go and hang out with some people who we were working with closely over in Saudi Arabia and she said that one more day wouldn't make that much difference, you know. I'm just really glad to be out of there.

I mean like I said earlier we knew that it could do the job and now we've really proven that it can do the job and whether or not it brings any more business or profitability to our company, that really doesn't matter to me that much at all. You know, obviously it would be a good thing, 'cause we're all stockholders. It's a private company, but just the chance to be there and see it means a lot more than dollars, I think.

The downside was that the Iraqi people could believe for a longer period of time the rhetoric of Saddam Hussein saying that we're winning the war and that we're doing all this damage and that allied forces aren't doing as much damage because there really wasn't much damage that they could measure because it was some building they never went into and that didn't really affect their day-to-day living so it sort of had some negative impact as far as Saddam could keep his rhetoric going longer and they would believe the stories longer just because they didn't get that collateral effect you'd normally get in the old war.

There was a purpose in not doing that. I'm not saying that you should bomb them to do that, but that it was a downside to it in that people don't even believe that the war's really going the wrong way. They're just going "We're winning!" and that's what they're telling us and CNN is lying to us or whatever. They won't believe all the British stories or the coalition stories. They can see it on the news—it's like, that must all be crap because look at this, we're all still living normally.

JIM IRWIN

Rank: Major
Service: Marine Corps
Duty: Mobilization Processing
Hometown: Palm Springs, California

I'm with the Mobilization Processing Center that's part of the IMADET, the Individual Mobilization Augment E Detachment here at Marine Corps base Camp Pendleton. And we were involved in processing all the SMCR and IRR Reservists to active duty. That's the Selective Marine Corps Reserves. Those are the active reservists from around the country that drill once a month and do two weeks active duty each year. The IRRs are Inactive Reservists that still have an obligated service time to the Marine Corps. We also process several of the combat replacement companies through the MPC and they were, they consisted of SMCR, IRR and some active duty Marine Corps and Navy personnel. A lot of corpsmen and doctors.

I was called in, actually, three times. Once for eight days in October, and then for six weeks November 7th to 18th of December, and then again I was activated for six months to a year starting the 19th of January. In civilian life, I'm a teacher full time. I teach an alternative education course. There's only two classes of that program at the high school and it was sort of a hardship not so much on me but on the kids that I teach. They need consistency and I was gone quite a bit of the school year. But I'm also the assistant varsity baseball coach at Palm Springs High School and that really threw a wrench into it.

But I got the, I actually got the activation call in my classroom and called my principal to tell him and he went a little ballistic. He didn't know really what to do. He had been expecting it, but then we got a good substitute in the classroom and he's doing a real good job. The, my position on the baseball team was filled by another guy that is doing a real good job and the baseball team's doing real well. But my wife is the one that really, really's been paying the price with me being gone and she's a teacher at Palm Springs High School also. But she's the one, when I called her, in her classroom, she had been expecting it just like everybody else, but it was on such a short notice. I was called on Tuesday morning and I was told to report on Thursday and of course the war started Wednesday afternoon so my wife and I were sitting at home Wednesday night just, you know, kind of clinging to each other, 'cause we really weren't sure what was going to happen.

We kind of figured that I would be here and when we ran out of people to process, we would be put into a final combat replacement company to go over to Saudi and we kind of figured that if this was going to go on for the long term like everyone had thought, this, I would have been going some time in April.

Financially, I make more money on active duty than I do as a school teacher. And so this has been a sort of a boon to me, but in a lot of the things I didn't go into my creditors and ask for any kind of delay in payments or ask for a reduction to the six percent because financially I could handle it. I know a lot of people that it's killing them.

Well we have a physician who is a reservist from the Midwest. He's come in on active duty and he's been our primary medical officer in the mobilization processing center and he, I guess he's just kind of written off his practice until he can get home. We have another sergeant who just signed a big consultation contract with IBM. He's a computer wizard and he's, his whole business is going down the drain right now, but I think their motivation was excellent.

For the most part, I mean, as I was seeing the faces of the people going through, what shocked me the most was the youth. They look just a little bit older than the kids I teach. But these, most of them were the SMCRs, they were coming right out of active duty. A lot of the active duty kids that we were getting were right out of the school of infantry so they were young, but the motivation of the reservists was outstanding. These guys were ready to go. And the delay in getting some of the IRRs into training was a demoralizing factor. They were, they felt like they were just here to sit around and now we've processed all of them to go back home and I think they're really happy to be gone.

I was a reservist on active duty back in the early '70s and was released from active duty in '75 and stayed most of the time here at Camp Pendleton. Of course, I did basic school at Quantico, Virginia; Supply School at Camp LeJeune, North Carolina. But I was stationed here for just about 18 months.

The only thing that I've heard is that the front elements moved so fast that the supply was just strained and couldn't keep up with them and sometimes they had to wait for it to catch up. It was there. That was one of the things that I feel was delayed. We could have kicked this thing off a long time ago, but the logistics wasn't in place yet. And I may be wrong in that, but it, a front line unit won't go anywhere without the logistics behind it to support it and there's a lot of people that say for every man on the front lines there's 15 to 20 behind him supporting him and that's a massive undertaking. The first floor service support group here at Camp Pendleton put together a massive support. At one point there were millions of MREs on this base. Those are the Meals Ready to Eat. They had all been mounted out and sent to Saudi Arabia.

The MREs are procured through the supply system, but then there was a new test undertaken for a new MRE that is pretty much something you can buy right here in the commissary or out in the local supermarkets that is something like top shelf and it's basically the same thing. Just heat it up and it's ready to go.

We've been hearing all kinds of things about some of the reserves that are still over in Saudi that won't be coming back immediately, some of the others that are in Okinawa that, we have two infantry battalions and four artillery batteries in Okinawa that won't be coming back sometime until August. I've also heard that personally we'll probably be kept on active duty until the end of September just to make sure that everything is completed and then we'll be writing after-action reports.

My job is secure. My principal, I've already talked to him about it and I talked to my wife and she's talked to him also. My concerns were that when I got back I was going to be reassigned somewhere else. It's, it would be quite a shock to go from teaching high school students to teaching sixth graders and that could happen. That would be an undesirable situation but I've been told that I will probably not only get my job back, but I'll get my own classroom that I gave up.

I wasn't married when I was on active duty. So this was something completely new for both of us. She's been doing everything by herself. I kind of compare it to she's working two full time jobs teaching at the high school and then coming home and handling the two children. She's been working real hard and she's been paying a price not only emotionally, psychologically, but also physically. She's working with a bad back. She's thrown her back out three times now in the past two months so she's got some limitations now. She's trying to do everything all at the same time.

The IMADET here at Camp Pendleton has a complex primary function. First we do special projects for the commanding general and the staff, the assistant chiefs of staff, and then the mobilization processing center has been the number one priority to get it ready to go and it was, it had never been tested like this before. It had only been used just to, well, we had run students through it, using dummy record books and we would find mistakes in those, but it had never really been tested like this.

We make sure that their orders have them reporting to the right base. We initially screen their, we screen their records for completeness in an administrative unit that was part of the warrior training command and then the individual would come over to the MPC and we would take the individual through 12 stations that consisted of medical records screening, shots, and so on.

ANTHONY S. ROBBINS

Rank: Sergeant
Service: Air Force
Duty: Civil Engineering
Hometown: Sanford, Michigan

I'm in a civil engineering squad, I'm out of Myrtle Beach, South Carolina. And we went there to set up a camp and maintain it. And I'm a power production troop, so I went there and helped, me and eight other guys. We built a power plant, and then maintained the power plant.

They sent in the generators, and we ran all the cables, both exterior electricians and interior electricians. Then we supplied power to that whole Tent City, which supplied power to about—close to ten thousand people. About eight hundred tents. If sirens went off, we'd hit the bunkers, we didn't shut the power off. If there would have been any kind of chemical agents detection, we would have shut it off, that way it doesn't get in the air-conditioning, you know, inside the tents and stuff. But in the meantime, if you don't have any power, you couldn't broadcast over the PA system, so you had to have the power on.

I got there August 20th. What stands out in my mind, I'm a newlywed, so—eleven months. I spent my first anniversary over there. And two weeks after I get there I get a letter from her, she says, oh, we're going to have our first baby, so that's why I'm coming home now. She's due in about six weeks, so . . .

They had telephone lines hooked up, the Mars system and the MCC, AT&T, it was easy to call. It's expensive to call, but I could call her every day if I wanted to.

I felt good about it. And I—let's put it this way, this was the first time in my Air Force career that I was actually proud of being in the Air Force. I'm serious, because our squadron, we just put together that camp, and then we had—we had flushing toilets out in the desert, you know, and we paved roads, you know, we did everything out there, you know, we ran—everybody had air-conditioning in their tents, and when it got cold, heat. Everybody had their own little light bulb they can turn on and off. It was great.

And you know, as a team, it all came together finally, you know. We trained for it, you know, every three months we have exercises and stuff that we train for it, and everybody has a little piece, carpenters, electricians, plumbers, whatever. If you put it all together, you can build up a city.

I had good job satisfaction at home, it's just that I . . . it wasn't—see, I wasn't planning making the Air Force my career, so I wasn't that gung ho about it. You know, I wasn't that really proud of being in the Air Force. But then, you know, that's what the service is all about, you know, defend the country or you go to war or whatever, and we finally did it since I've been in it. And I felt good about it.

Like I said earlier, my wife is due in six weeks, so I'm going to take a couple of weeks off when I get back. Go back and work for a couple of weeks, then I'm going to take a month off, because I've got a lot of leave saved up. But I want to have a good month off, so when around the time she's due . . .

STEPHANIE L. ANAYA

Rank: Sergeant
Service: Army
Duty: Nutritionist
Hometown: Cranesville, West Virginia

I'm stationed at Fort Carson, Colorado, in Colorado Springs. I'm twenty-eight years old. I'm a 91 Mike Hospital Food Service. We make special diets, you know, if somebody has been shot or if they are wounded and they can't have regular food, we make it so that they can be fed through the stomach or through their throat.

We were following the 24th Infantry. Until they were sent to an EVAC hospital. We would keep them 72 hours. A MASH unit keeps patients 72 hours, stabilizes them, and then sends them to an EVAC. Another company next to us, a big MASH, they took care of the primary care for the patients. We were the standby that we would have to move into Kuwait. But then the cease-fire came, and so we didn't.

The hardships, well, the guys in the service, they treated us like soldiers, they didn't—you know, it wasn't like, you're a female and you're weaker. They treated us as part of the team. And they would—you know, it was like a field exercise, except that it was a little bit more real. It was more intense. But as far as being treated as part of the team, we were treated equal.

We knew where we fit in. You know, we knew that we were—we weren't the first increment of hospital to move forward. We were going to be the second increment, that if they were overloaded—we sent a lot of our people in our hospital on a fast team, which they were right there in the front. They were the front-line soldiers. So a lot of our soldiers were the fast team. Where we had a—it was only a one-bed OR, and then they were treated in. Now, if we would have had to set up, we would have been behind the fast team, and then we would have had a four-bed OR.

We had colonels, officers there. We were a complete hospital, a field hospital. We had everything. We would treat patients, like I said, if they were shot, or if you were a diabetic, or if your mouth was, you know, been blowed up or something, we would make meals that you could get enough, we could sustain you.

We had it with us at all times. We have an MKT, it's called, it's a Mobile Kitchen Trailer. And with all the, you know, all this stuff to prepare meals. Plus we had dietary meal supplements. You know, you couldn't just give someone an MRE if they were going to—you know, if they couldn't eat. We had to provide meals so that they could make it.

To me, when I realized it was real, when I was driving up into Iraq—before I thought it was just kind of like a field exercise. But when I drove into Iraq, and I seen all the tanks and all the guys with the M16s on the back of their vehicles, then I knew it was real. That's what's going to stick in my mind. And being in Cement City when the Scuds were blowing above us. Then that's when I knew it was real, it wasn't like a field exercise.

We were on guard when there was a Scud attack and then the Patriots going up—and I was on guard, and we seen them going past our compound. I couldn't judge the distance. They were above us. But they said that they were probably about—I think they said twenty miles from where they actually hit the Patriots. It kind of sounded like the Fourth of July, because you could just see Boom! And then Boom-Boom-Boom! Because the Patriots hit.

It was so far — by the time we realized it, we heard the Patriot going off, you know, being sent, and then by the time it hit the Scud, we just heard Boom-Boom-Boom. Like the Fourth of July. Just kind of like a bottlecap rocket, you know, shooting out of a bottle. You see that little flairing behind it. That was all.

You know, it was—they broke it up so that it was male and female areas. You know, they treated us good. What they could do in the field environment, you know. You had your privacy. I actually get over there the 4th of January. We learned that we can really work as a team. See, we had a lot of new soldiers and a lot of officers, that we had never worked with before. They were just in our unit, but we never worked with them actually, that we worked together as a team. It wasn't officer and enlisted, it was just together.

If we had moved into Kuwait and actually set up hospital, we would have had two Saudi Arabian MPs and some American MPs, because they could translate for our patients and stuff like that.

These are night fatigues I'm wearing. Night desert fatigues that they gave you. You wear them over you— we call them chocolate chips, but it's desert fatigues, but we called them chocolate chips. You'd wear them over— they were good for the night, you can't detect them, you can't see them at night. Plus they keep the sand off you. But not everybody got the clothing, you know, not all units received the clothing that they were supposed to. They gave it to the front-line people. You were supposed to bring a second issue. Like we were told to bring a pair that we wear, and then a secondary pair, so you would have that in case you couldn't get supplies that you needed.

We were told on our packing list, we had, you know, supplies, and then secondary supplies that we had brought ourselves. We were supposed to have been activated in September. But things went so well that they didn't activate us actually until January. They had other MASH units there.

I want people to know that women can do it. I mean, you know, we weren't the front-line soldiers, and we didn't fight actual combat like these guys have seen. But you have it in you. It's in there, in the training that you learn. It's there. Women have the right, just like the men do there. They're essential, you need them.

You don't realize it when you're getting the training, you think, you know, this is silly, I don't know why I'm learning this. But when it actually gets down to it, it all comes back and it does fit in that you need it. A lot of it, I was like, now I know why I learned to dig bunkers and dig foxholes. Before, I thought, this is stupid, let's get in the car and drive away. But now you know why it's essential.

One thing I got to tell people, that if you're not ready to leave your family and go and do what you put your hand up to do—a lot of people join the military because they thought of education, and they didn't realize that war could happen. If you're not ready to really sit down and say, I could possibly go to war, then don't do it. Some soldiers said, I joined the Army for the military education. But you can go to war.

I have a fiancé that we were both in the same unit. And we had to leave our son back. And it was hard, because if something happened to both of us, then he would just be with my grandparents. My family. So that part was hard. But it was kind of good, too, because we were together. He's ten months old. When my parents got him, he was seven months old. And now he's ten months old.

We were both in the same unit. I have emergency leave. So I have to go back and take care of my son. But if you're not—when you raise your hand, if you're not ready to go to war, then don't raise your hand. Because I thought myself that it would never happen. I came in for education. But I never thought in my wildest dreams that it would be war. So when you get ready to raise your hand, think that there could be the possibility of war.

We're not married, we're just—you know, in the process of getting married. But it doesn't—even if you're married, it doesn't matter because you're an individual. It doesn't matter if you have a dependent. And you raised your hand. The Army didn't issue you children. They issued you an M-16 and some clothes.

If you're a single parent, a female, or a male with a single child, and there's no one else to provide for your child, you have the opportunity—the Army offers you that to get out of the service, because it would be called hardship. And no one else can provide for your child. So the Army does not say, you have no choice, you have to go. You have the opportunity to say, I want out, because I have no one to take care of my family. It's not like your sex, you know, you have the choice. So anyone that's here, it's their own choice. It's not because the Army made them.

EMIL C. DESBIENS

Rank: Lance Corporal
Service: Marine Corps
Duty: Infantry
Home State: New Jersey

I'm from originally New Jersey and this month, the end of this month I've got two years in the Marine Corps. Two years left to go, hopefully more if I can make it a career, but when the ground war first started I was pretty excited. They were saying since we didn't go when the air war started we would go when the ground war started and that excited me because I wanted to get out of here. I had some problems back in New Jersey, a lot of things I need to straighten out in my life. I thought if I could go over there and do my job I would have my mind work, you know, my body would be working therefore my mind would be working and I wouldn't be half as bad.

I went over to Okinawa. I was there for a year. I came back in December. I came here with a group of others and we've been here since. When we first got here they said don't bother unpacking, you'll be going out right away. We said, well, that's good, okay. And then when we didn't go out for a while we said, well, what's going on, can we go? And they told us, no, we couldn't go forward because the commander of Pacific Forces said no, no one's going forward unless they get called by name, if they need your MOS, and then I found out my MOS, the people in my MOS, my Military Occupational Specialty.

People in my MOS weren't doing their job, they were doing other jobs. Which was just as well because they were training. They were getting other training which is good. The more training you have the better off you are. And a friend of mine who came back with me from Okinawa—we arrived in L.A. on the 14th of December—he checked in here on the 17th of December, which was a Monday. He was gone that Friday to Saudi Arabia. He shipped out right away. He was hurting in a bad way 'cause his father died like two, a week before we came home, actually. And he got sent right out.

I haven't had the opportunity to talk to anyone over there. I've had the opportunity to talk to a friend of mine from Okinawa who came here en route to Saudi about a month and a half ago. But as far as living in a foxhole and stuff, I've done that, you know, in the field before. It's an experience. Dirty, nasty, and if it rains on you it's no fun.

We weren't able to go, right? We tried to go, my friends and I, we all tried. We asked to go. It doesn't make a whole lot of difference right now. But we did request to go. We're upset and sad that we didn't get the opportunity to go. We're disappointed that we didn't get to go. But as my friend's wife put it, you know, we spent a year on Okinawa, we did our job over there. We came back here and we did the job that the Marine Corps told us to do. We did it to the best of our ability and on top of that, we're marines and we should be proud of the fact that we're part of the fighting force that was there.

CHUCK WEATHERMAN

Rank: Corporal
Service: Marine Corps
Duty: Infantry
Hometown: Camp Pendleton, California

We were . . . our job was to clear the trenches. And work our way up to Kuwait International Airport and gradually Kuwait City. As we were clearing the last trench, most of them surrendered, came out of the trench, waving white flags so's we let 'em advance forward so we could search the POWs themselves. We waited until they got up close enough.

How shall I say this? Kind of hard to explain what we— we set up on line, saw to our POW search and handling teams, me being a M60 gunner I was laying 20 meters back to the right, cover fire for them if they need it. And as the POWs got close enough to be searched, they had left a mortar team back in the trench and started dropping mortar rounds on us. One of them landed a few feet from my head. Caught some shrapnel in the neck. We were roughly thirty klicks in when it happened.

My body went kind of numb. It took me a couple of seconds to feel it after my body went numb. I figured I was hit, then I felt a real, hot burning sensation in my neck and I knew I was hit.

There were six of us hit by the mortar attack. No Iraqis got hit even though they were all around us surrendering; we were the only ones that got hit. They were pretty scared. They obviously didn't know that they were going to attack us 'cause they were all jumping down looking around. They thought we were going to kill 'em.

We didn't meet resistance from these Iraqis or from the first breach. They were just, most of them didn't want to fight, they just wanted to surrender.

We took real good care of 'em. They were well fed and well treated. They weren't abused in any way. They were at the same field hospital that I was. They were getting the same medical treatment that we were.

Before we went in, we were pretty close to the border. We were watching the light shows, watching the planes fly over, watching the tracers from the enemy guns shooting at the planes. We had designated SCUD holes we would get into whenever they would appear, a SCUD coming in our direction we would all get in those SCUD holes. As far as I know, none came near us.

DWAYNE R. BISHOP

Rank: Sergeant
Service: Marine Corps
Duty: Infantry
Hometown: Edgartown, New Jersey

My original hometown is in Jersey, Edgartown, New Jersey, it's a small farming town. Once I got into Saudi Arabia, I really didn't know what to expect. I knew it was going to be a desert land and everything like that but it was a change and when we did start the air war when we were up north of Saudi Arabia, we had—I was on post one night with a buddy of mine and we took incoming rocket fire and I—it was quite a scare because it was within I'd say a little under a mile and the rocket fire was so large and intense that it was real big explosions.

We knew something was going on but we didn't know exactly what and I was watching the artillery barrage of Khafji because we could see the artillery going in to Khafji. And I was talking to my buddy and you know we were just talking back and forth saying, "You know, they're really hitting Khafji hard," and then we saw four red flashes and I looked to him and I said, "You know, my God, this stuff's coming at us! That's incoming!" And then we had radioed it in and not but about 20 seconds later we had the impacts not more than I'd say less than a mile away.

We didn't hear anything. The only thing we saw was the launch of the rockets themselves. The initial flash and then when I'd said, "That's incoming!" because it looked like it was coming towards us and then we didn't see or hear anything until the actual explosion of the rounds and the flash of the rounds.

I'd say they were launched from about let's say a good 40-50 miles away. The night, it was a real clear night so we could see a lot of stuff. In the compound that we were in there was approximately 340 of us. It was the headquarters element that was in the compound.

The compound that we were in, it was all dug in holes and we had our CRC set up and the whole area was spread out. And where I was it was on a bunker post. We were just watching the forward area to make sure that nobody was coming in or make sure that we didn't get overran or anything like that from any Iraqi forces.

The training that we received over here was excellent. We went through a lot of desert survival classes, a lot of desert training. The EOD people, they came down, they gave us very intense classes on mines and booby traps. They shows us the different kinds of mines that the Iraqis had bought or acquired through different sources and the training was very outstanding.

We had started training with the chemical protective suit back in Hawaii, which is where I'm stationed. And the training once we—when we were still in K Bay the training wasn't real intense because we didn't know the actual intensity of what he was going to utilize over here. Once we got over here and found out that he had so many SCUD missiles and that he could launch chemical capabilities from his artillery rounds and stuff like that our training on chemical protection I mean increased quite a bit.

A lot of things were running through my mind. Number one I didn't think we would come over here to Saudi Arabia, because of where we are located. And then once we did get to Saudi Arabia we found out that it was right in our area of operations and I just didn't think we would go. But we did go and it was a lot of mixed emotions. You know I'd . . . sometimes I didn't feel like being there because I thought it was just, you know, just a bunch of bull and, you know, felt like, you know, "Hey look, they want to fight themselves, let them fight themselves. You know it's not our war."

And then after reading some of the intel reports and different things like that, it did become our war, because it wasn't over oil anymore. It was over power and the way I looked at it then was if Saddam Hussein kept getting power, and more power, and he would have taken Saudi Arabia by force and he could have, then we would have been fighting a bigger war than what we did.

I handled two different sets of POWs. The first set was a tank brigade that gave up. And I was part of the security element that went out to pick them up. We saw their tanks, most of them were T-55s and T-62s that I had seen. I didn't see very many T-72 Russian tanks. The condition that they were in, they looked like they haven't had showers in weeks. I mean they were real dirty. They smelled bad. Some of them were injured from either their own negligence on things or being in a fire fight with our allied forces. That was the first that they came across. The second set, we were going through I think it was Begon oil fields, and it was at night and the wind was really bad and we were driving along on a convoy and my gunner which was up on top of the turret saw a white flag out off to the right and you know we stopped to see what it was.

And we had noticed this flag and we had stopped to see what it was and it was 300 Iraqis giving up. And some of them were, well, all of them were very hungry. They said that they were walking for three to four hours without any food or water. They didn't have any weapons on them.

We were expecting anything because going up into Kuwait and all the POWs that we were hearing were Iraqis that were giving up we were just, we were prepared for war and we were going in with such a force that they were. I don't think the Iraqis were prepared for what the United States had to put against them. Because with the Iran/Iraq war, it was push and shove back and forth both ways. With the coalition forces and the Iraqis, we had hit them, we kept driving in. And I don't think that they were prepared for that.

At first we didn't see very much of the air bombing going on because we were still in Saudi Arabia on the other side of the border of Kuwait and we really didn't see that much. We heard a lot of it. We heard the A-1 fire going off and stuff like that. Once we got in and saw some of the air bombardment going on, it was still off in the distance, but we could see the flashes of light. In my mind the air war was essential to soften up the targets for the ground war because I think that if the air didn't go in when it did, and we would have attacked by the ground, we would have probably taken more casualties and we wouldn't have gotten as far as fast.

The only people that we had attached to us was our SIOPS people and there was two Kuwaiti officers in that, but that was the only multinational forces that I have dealt with.

SHELLY TOM

Rank: Senior Airman E4
Service: Air Force
Duty: Food Service
Hometown: Los Angeles, California

I'm stationed at McChord Air Force Base in Washington state. I'm 22 years old. I was in food services. I cooked for the troops, supported—I was in support. We cooked with B rations, which is you know the military—everything is in cans and everything. Dehydrated food. And we cooked for about 15,000 people out there. We had five dining facilities in our compound and we prepared three hot meals a day—breakfast, dinner and the night meal. In Riyadh, Saudi Arabia.

The first SCUD attack, all I remember was throwing on my gear quickly and praying. What I thought was happening was I thought bombs were hitting us because the Patriot missiles were going off and I didn't know what the booms were, so I just felt anxiety and scared and I started praying.

We had about three weeks notice. Where I was at it was very nice. We lived in villas and we had six facilities, showers, bathrooms. We had no problems. You see, we were in the capital of Saudi Arabia. So we didn't have the static a lot of the other troops had.

I think what impressed me the most was the way everybody pulled together. I worked with the nationals from Bangladesh and Sri Lanka—the surrounding countries around there. It was a little hard. They were really nice. They liked us a lot but it was hard to speak with them. But that was a hard thing because I felt bad for them. They thought that they were going to die because they had no protection. And we did. They were so scared the whole time and that was hard.

We officially issued them gas masks and stuff. When it first started they didn't come to work at all. But we told them they'd be safer here with us then to be out there.

CHARLES R. WOODS, JR.

Rank: Staff Sergeant
Service: Marine Corps
Duty: Infantry
Hometown: Kailua, Hawaii

I'm a platoon sergeant in an infantry platoon. Our whole experience was just prepping for the war. And it was kind of, the actual Gulf war days was kind of a let down. Because we'd spent a little over six months—especially me kind of being the grim reaper type of individual, you know, if you mess this up or screw this up you're going to die—and nothing happened.

I'm not the head of the platoon. Between a lieutenant, a commissioned officer and myself, we run the platoon. He makes the decision and I enforce the decisions. We've got thirty men.

We processed in the neighborhood of 4,000 POWs. What we had to do—as they came in and they just came in like . . . formations of people—saying, "George Bush number one." They were just letting us know that they were giving up. Not all of them had white flags. They were saying George Bush number one and all kinds of bad things about Saddam.

What we had to do was, first we separated all the officers and the enlisted people. Most of them tore the rank insignia off so they couldn't be identified. But there's always—there's English speaking people all over the place, a lot of guys were like, "I'm from Chicago, where you guys been?" They would come up—there was an exact case like that.

A guy came up to me and said "I'm from Chicago. I was here visiting my family and they just conscripted me and sent me down here to fight and I've just been waiting for you guys." The guys that spoke English for the most part were usually who the officers were. Most of the officers did speak English. We would separate them so nobody could take charge if something went wrong and then we had to strip-search everybody. We heard rumors that another unit was going through one of these and an Iraqi had stuck a grenade under his armpit and blew himself up as well as the marine. But it turned out later to be false. But in the middle of a war situation you don't know. We strip-searched every one of them, went through all their clothes, all that good stuff. And then courted them into a pen where we could get them some food and water. That's what they wanted. They needed food and water bad.

I was surprised at how old they were. Our forces probably average 20-21 years old. These guys probably average 30-35. Rag-tag and ratty uniforms compared to our guys. The biggest trouble was in the shoes. It looks like they had enough shirts and trousers for everybody, but we saw guys in all kinds of civilian shoes and cleats and some had boots. It was wild.

No doubt about it. The air war won this one. They wouldn't have given up without us going in. But without them doing the air war the way they did it, it would have been nasty. The only thing we saw was a few SCUDs going over there at night, but when we were still at Khafji we could see stuff coming in but we were never in any danger.

It looked like just a fiery star ball. We were on a guide post up there during the air war and you could see the Patriots hitting them through the NVG, that's night vision goggles, and you could see them light up the sky real bright.

You know, we spent almost seven months in the desert—maybe for a month of that we had a tent. It got cold—starting in about November, it got cold. We had sleeping bags and all that kind of stuff. And we had camouflage nets. We use them to camouflage the tanks and stuff. We had those over us. It helped keep us hidden.

Food and water we got plenty of. We got showers probably once a week to once every two weeks. The supply units won the war just as much as the air war did. Because we had everything we needed when we needed it. Like I said, we were front line troops and we would bitch because we didn't get our uniforms in time or our covers in time, or certain boot on time—little things like that. But we had what we needed to fight and win a war.

JOHN R. ROBERTS

Rank: Master Sergeant
Service: Air Force
Duty: Medivac Technician
Hometown: Anchorage, Alaska

I'm an Air Force brat. I'm one of those itinerant, vagrant children, don't have a home. If I had to go some place tomorrow I'd probably go back to Anchorage, Alaska, though, and I've been here at the 2nd Air Evac now for a year and a half and the last six months has been down range in the Gulf area.

My primary duties at the first location where I was were that of a line flier. I was an air medical evacuation technician. I was crew member on about eight missions out of Dhahran and I crewed about eight missions out of Dhahran as either Charge Medical Tech or Second Medical Technician. The job is to provide inflight patient care for returning sick and injured American troops and we were flying from Saudi back here to Germany, and we would average anywhere from one to 60 patients on a mission and that ran from the time that we first started deploying troops to the Gulf through today. We're still moving patients.

I was not in direct contact with any patients who were combat casualties. Most of my patient movements were prior to the air war, ground war beginning. I did recover POWs after I had moved to Bahrain when they flew the U.S. POWs back in from Riyadh. I was there when the first ten came in, also helped recover the next package two days, three days later.

They looked to be markedly thin. Everybody has said that when we've come back we've lost weight, well, it isn't that noticeable to us, but they looked thin. I mean, we could tell the difference there. They were, they had obvious weight loss, they appeared to be very aware and very intense. They knew that they were back home even in Bahrain. They were there with Americans and I shook hands and spoke very briefly with Colonel Eberly and it was very obvious that he was quite on top of what was going on. He looked very happy to be back among friends.

During the first four months that we were over there, it was very surprising the number of people that we saw that were deployed because the unit's deployed. And medical history was kind of, didn't seem to have been a consideration. The unit's going, so you're going even though a good sharp doc would tell you today, "You ought not be going." We did take a lot of people back to Germany like that.

As an Air Force medic, I really was never in the field, per se. In Saudi, I was living in a tent city on a fixed facility base. We ate in a chow hall. We had two hots and a Meal-Ready-to-Eat a day and life there was pretty good. It was very communal and among our group we were just waiting for missions to fly and when we weren't flying missions if there wasn't something else to otherwise occupy our time right locally, we were in a down mode. That was not bad duty at all. Then at the end of four months I moved from Saudi to Bahrain and helped to open a new air evac hub and the facilities got markedly better. We were living in a four-story villa and we had catered meals twice a day. We still had the option on the one MRE, but we were in the middle of a Shiite neighborhood with absolutely no security other than what we provided ourselves off the rooftop and that was kind of different.

The Bahraini seemed a lot warmer and a lot more friendly towards us, but I think that's just a basic cultural difference. The Bahrainis are a lot more westernized than the Saudis are anyway. They're not nearly as religiously conservative or fundamental as the Saudis. But when the war was over, when they finally declared a halt of hostilities, the Bahrainis were all over the streets. They were parading in their cars, waving flags and so on. And we were still in a Threat Con Charlie situation there in our villa. We were not allowed out, we couldn't go other than to work from the villa and we were pretty confined. But they ran these parades around the block that the villa was on, honking horns and waving flags and shouting up and waving at us. And it gave us a very strong sense that they knew who we were, why we were there, and they were very grateful that we had done so. We had a reception a week or so later over at one of the hotels hosted by the Kuwaitis and pretty much everyone you talked to was very openly grateful. "Thank you very much for what your country has done." "Thank you for being here." And it was a good feeling.

The "Any Serviceman" letter, everybody got those. And I've got a penpal from Missouri now, a 12-year-old gal. She plays volleyball and babysits. And she was writing me and sending me packages for six months solid. And I've never seen this gal face to face yet. And she's a peach. And everybody had a class of third graders or a church group or something that was, kept pumping them good stuff all the time. Packages, letters, it was terrific. We knew the whole time that America was with us in spite of the article or two that you'd see now and again in Stars and Stripes or on CNN or whatever we were getting on TV that led you to believe that there were pockets of the '60s still around. We knew that America wasn't buying off on that as a whole.

The day after the ground war started I believe it was, or two days later, it was the day after the fires had been set, I had to take one of my folks up to a more forward location in Saudi. He was going to be giving some inservice on medical equipment to another air evac unit and when we left Bahrain, it was a nice day. I was wearing sun glasses. And we arrived up at this other location on the Saudi coast about three hours north about noontime and it was like driving into the biggest midwestern thunderstorm you'd ever seen. I mean the sky was black all the way down to the horizon and it was like any minute now it's going to turn really, really ugly. And that was smoke out of Kuwait. It just blackened the sky. It was horrible.

When we moved into Bahrain, there had been an advance party. We were all hooked up with, we had group of air med crews, co-located with an ASF—air medical staging flight—also co-located eventually with a mobile staging facility and then there were various Army and Navy hospitals as well as Bahraini military hospitals that were also around to be giving support except patients that we brought in, pumped patients out back into the system to Europe. So when we came in, the ASF was already in place, but there was nothing as far as the air evac function so we got there on the 5th of January. It was before the war. There was not a lot of sense of urgency on the part of the Bahrainis at that time. They had talked about, "When the war starts, you have this, this and this."

But the war hadn't started yet. And so therefore none of that was available to us and the sense of urgency just wasn't quite there as yet with the Bahrainis. They had told us that we would be able to set up our operation in the main terminal of the international airport, but since the war hadn't started, "Well, we're still an airport and until then you don't have any of this facility." So we were operating off of pallets and out of a large Conex paint locker over at a Navy facility, the raider base. A great bunch of people. They gave us everything they could and they didn't have anything to give away. They were wonderful folks. We really appreciated all that we got from them.

But then as soon as they switched Desert Shield to Desert Storm, the Bahrainis were falling all over themselves. We went from pallets and Conexes to being fully operational in the terminal with all of our equipment set up and ready to receive and send patients in about 12 hours.

There were very few Air Force on Bahrain. And so we were very much a low profile outfit in an island basically that was Naval ASU and the desert ducks and raider base over on the flight line and so we kind of stayed low profile but nobody if ever they found out that you were Air Force or weren't Marines or weren't Navy, they really didn't care. I mean we were all there for a reason and that was far more important than giving anybody flak about the fact that their hat was funny looking. What I thought was even more noticeable than that because you almost expected that amongst U.S. forces, was how little garbage there was back and forth among nationalities. The Brits—the Brits were great to work with. They had a British war hospital co-located with our ASF and those people were fabulous. Really good to work with. The New Zealanders worked in the same medical facility down at Fleet 6 hospital with our Navy personnel. If you had it and they needed it, well, they had it because you did and vice versa. It was very much a coalition effort.

We got our daily word twice a day of course in Bahrain through CNN. We had CNN feed there on the island and so you could go to any floor in the villa and watch TV and that's all there was to watch was CNN. Prior to that when I was back in Saudi, we had CNN late at night on the Armed Forces Network channel, but our newspapers were running anywhere from four to seven days late and I quit seeing newspapers once I got to Bahrain. But we stayed pretty up to date in Bahrain with CNN.

One plug I would like to make for communications and for administrative support in general, I found out just how incredibly important it is. Since we were not located on a military installation, we didn't have any of that. And trying to stay in touch with people who were back in Saudi who were running the show for us there in Bahrain, it was real difficult. You couldn't always get through on the Bahraini to Saudi commercial landlines and routing messages had to go through some place else and your priority one became somebody else's priority 15 because they already had their one through 14s and you weren't going to bump them out and so that, yes, suddenly 19 years of peacetime communications understanding got real clarified with six months out in the desert. It got a lot more important because it always works. You're always on base. Suddenly we weren't on base and it didn't work for stink. A lot of times.

Again having been in Saudi, and being so close to that location while we were in Bahrain, we weren't completely out of the loop. I mean, if there was something we needed, we could send a truck and somebody to go over to Dhahran and get stuff that we required. But if that hadn't been available to us, I think on Bahrain we would have been hanging out there dry. 'Course our medical equipment, all we needed do was send out a message again back up to Riyadh and tell them, "We're out of business. We've just launched two missions, all of our oxygen equipment is gone and we've got crews sitting here. We've got everything else, but we can't provide oxygen to patients." Zoom! It was there the next day. They couldn't afford to have a hub closed down. So we managed; regardless of what sort of problems should have been there the logistics lines made themselves work.

There were no Iraqi POWs came into Bahrain at all that I'm aware of. We did have dealings with the Bahrainis themselves with the Bahraini Defense Force and in fact some of my folks were teaching a litter lifting class for BDF litter bearers. And that was very interesting because there was the obvious language barrier—my guys didn't speak Arabic, and most of their guys didn't speak English—so everything was done through a translator and then in the second class that was taught, we were about 20 minutes into the class and we had a SCUD alert. And so we confirmed that, yes, there's an inbound SCUD alert, we went into our chemical posture as we're trained to do and these Bahrainis they're getting wide-eyed and weird. "Oh God, the Americans are putting on their chem masks."

And so once we got chemmed up, we got them calmed down, and started helping them get their chem gear on, and the sirens are still sounding, they haven't called the all clear yet, and the guy I had teaching the class he says, "Well, what do we do?" "Continue." So he got everybody's attention, got them all sat back down, and everybody's sitting there in chem masks and stuff and he said, "You could have to lift litters wearing masks so this is good training. This is good practice. We'll work like this."

And we finished up the lecture portion of the class in chem masks. It was great.

Our area there at the flight line, we had blast walls built pretty much where we were. It was a hardened shelter as far as anything other than direct hits. The British Corps of Engineers had come in on Air War Day One and erected massive concrete bunker walls in front of the arrival area of the airport where we were set up. So, like I say, we were for everything other than a direct hit we had the best bunker that could have been going. We had no glass problems, we had no flying objects coming through. It would have taken a solid shot to have done us any damage. The classroom basically was protected in that area. So we're as sheltered as we're going to get so continue with the class.

In probably every combat experience and every war experience the further down the line from the command end you are, the more screwed up it seems to be. And I wasn't quite exactly on the tail end of the line, but I was by no means real close to the command end either. And so we saw a lot of things that, gee, it didn't seem like anybody up top was thinking real straight to us. But regardless of poor input, garbled input, or no input, the people that worked the mission made the mission work.

If we got no heads up that a plane was coming in, we still recovered the patients. If we got no heads up that a mission was going out, we still had the crew out there. We received the patients, put them on the airplane, and got the mission launched on time. The people made it work and I was working with guards, I was working with reservists, and there were only a half dozen of us active duty there at that location in Bahrain and again we all got together, we did the mission, we made it work. And I was very proud to have worked with all of them. It was wonderful.

There were some who were career reservists who had a very clear picture of what was happening and where they figured into it. There were also some who were either very new reservists or very deluded who thought that they were in the reserves to be going to school and making a weekend paycheck occasionally. And it was more than one time I heard somebody say, "Well, I shouldn't be here, I'm a reservist." Well, they now by this point understand that that's what the reserves are for. There are not enough active duty personnel to take care of all contingencies. And they are an important part of what we have to have in order to make our military system work.

And it was a rude awakening for several and they woke up very strong once they caught on that they were there and that they were going to work, they worked like gangbusters. But it bummed a few of them out right at first to be getting off the bus and being there and "I've got a class tomorrow morning at 9:00. I really shouldn't be here." "No, you're here, bud. And don't worry about class—you can catch up when you get home."

BARRETT F. RICHEY

Rank: Civilian
Duty: Computer Technician
Hometown: Chantilly, Virginia

Well, initially, probably the biggest impact on me was just getting there. The MAAC flight over in the freezing cold C-141 was quite interesting, trying to keep warm enough to keep from freezing to death. From Germany is where I took the MAAC flight, but I flew from Washington, D.C. the night before. And so while the flight over was great from Washington 'cause it was a business class United and so forth and then from there to, waiting 12 hours at the German airbase and finally getting on a C-141. A big difference: webbed seats, about 30 degrees inside the holding area and men dressed in all the military garb and me as a civilian with just you know my notebook and so forth and everyone else with rifles. You know you're really getting into something when you're doing that.

And then we landed in Dhahran which is where all the sorties were taking off from and I got there about the middle of the first, middle of the second week of February so there were, they had already been going full blast and so I got there about four in the morning and the planes, you know, the sorties were taking off every five minutes, you know, the jets. And where I had to stay for about five hours was right there at the air terminal. So I mean you could see all the planes lined up and the gassing them up and working on them right there inside the hangar. And so it's like from peaceful everyday life 24 hours ago to suddenly you know you might get SCUDed and all the jets taking off with the ordnance and so forth. So it was a big change.

We had a one-day training in sort of a gas mask, how to put that on and so forth, also how to deal with unexploded ordnances and so forth, just more of a survivability sort of training which was probably enough given that we were supposed to be stationed in Riyadh, not like up in Kuwait or you know getting ready to move in with the tanks or something. Once I got to Riyadh which was just later on that day, things almost, it just changed.

By the 14 or 15 or something of February it was more like the war seemed far away because it wasn't . . . I mean you had the occasional SCUD alert but you drove around in cars and you, you know, the people just doing everyday things and you dropped your laundry off. You know, it was just sort of everyday life even though there was a war going on it wasn't like that being up close to the front where they were getting SCUDed and so forth.

We did some traveling near the end actually after the ground war was basically finished to do some system upgrades and helping them pack their systems up to go home. But other than that, no, we spent, I spent the whole war in Riyadh, so we did get SCUDed a few times where, you know, the Patriots had to go up and take out the missiles and so forth, but I went down into the vault or whatever downstairs 'cause I was right there, next to it where other technicians were working. But other people were caught outside, but it just wasn't the same alarming thing that they talked about the first week 'cause the first week they didn't know if the Patriots were going to work or a lot of people probably didn't even hear of the Patriot before. And suddenly it was just "Oh, those'll take them out" so it wasn't, the urgency just didn't seem to be there like it was initially.

By the time I got there it was just like, "Well, the Patriots will take them out" and you just you know. I mean you still take shelter and you should still wear your gas mask, but it wasn't a sense of urgency like I'm sure there was initially because they didn't have that concept of "Well, those things will work." I mean, if you haven't seen them work yet, how can you know they're going to work.

There was a, on our way home from Riyadh we flew to Jedda and while we were on the plane we noticed a guy waiting for the plane that had a bandage where he didn't have a nose and a bandage was there and over his one eye. And we got to talking with another gentleman that was with him. And he was telling us he was a doctor, an Egyptian doctor from Baghdad that was caught and where he was working in a hospital part of the hospital was blown away and he was caught in the fire and they were taking him back to New York to get some reconstructive surgery I would imagine.

They said he was in a hospital so my guess is a civilian hospital that happened to be too close to some of the bombs. I mean, it's hard to say whether it was one of ours or some triple A fire. I mean they had stories where the triple A fire would spin around and like cut the top of a building off so it's hard to say, with so much going on over there but he, they missed a flight to, up to Paris so there was a reporter with them from the Boston Globe that was trying to figure out why someone didn't call ahead 'cause he requested someone to call ahead and hold the plane for this guy and so it went round and round for like two or three hours. It was fairly interesting just to see everyone trying to work together with the language barrier and so forth.

There was a lot of civilian contractors in the theater because of the sophistication of the systems, plus the fact that a lot of the systems there or over there weren't tested in this sort of a real environment and also the, "Gee, wouldn't it be nice if they could do these sort of things for us" and then being careful not to disrupt the normal functions of the system trying to add some functionality so that you could handle some of the cases that cropped up during the war. You can roll hardware off the pallet, but you can't get them coordinated to communicate what each of them needs to do in a day.

CONRAD A. LANGLEY

Rank: Commander
Service: Navy
Duty: S-3 pilot
Hometown: Spring Valley, California

I started out on the 2nd of August. We were just off the southern tip of India and we were headed for Diego Garcia and of course on the 2nd of August we turned and headed directly for the Persian Gulf. And we got up there alive about the 6th or 7th of August and stationed ourselves in the Gulf of Oman. Immediately we went into a very intense planning period, planning strikes, planning contingencies with the idea at that point of stopping Saddam Hussein from moving into Saudi Arabia. That was the first thing we looked at.

As things settled down and he started digging in, contingency planning proceeded along different lines. My squadron got immediately involved with the embargo and started flying daily sorties on surface ship interdiction, getting a radar picture of the area, surface ships, and going in and identifying each ship, and calling up and talking to the master of each ship, finding out what they were carrying and where they were going and where they were coming from. And if we had reason to believe that they were headed for Iraq and carrying embargoed items we would vector US Navy destroyers or cruisers in to conduct the boardings.

We were working 16-17 hours a day between the planning and the flying and planning the flights and the contingency planning. The ship was, the living conditions on the ship were not bad, not nearly as bad as guys living in the desert, in the sand, but the water was warmer so the ship's air-conditioning system wasn't, it still worked, but not as efficiently as if the water were cooler so—still the supply chain was pretty well established and the food stayed pretty decent. Probably the greatest hardship for the crew was the slow mail. The mail was running anywhere from four to six weeks behind and so people were having to put up with a lack of knowledge of what's going on back home and that's a hardship, not knowing what their families are doing.

Everyone was keyed up to doing their job, was preparing for the job that, everyone from the young fellas maintaining the airplane and my hat's really off to them. Those guys were working long, long hours—16, 17, 18 hours a day—working on the airplanes, preparing the airplanes for the worst, for having to go into battle. People on the ship were working hard practicing damage control. So morale in that sense was up, and the only detractor to morale was the mail. The fact that we weren't getting enough mail and we knew mail was out there. We had messages that mail was getting bogged down out there. Of course, we understood that because they had to fly parts and troops into the area. Other than that morale was extremely high.

Initially, the skies weren't too crowded because we were the only ones out there. And initially the airline traffic was still going on in the Gulf states there so that really didn't have too much of an effect. As we moved from early August into October, November with more and more Air Force squadrons arriving, it became more crowded. On our missions for interdicting the ships we were at low levels so we didn't have to worry too much about traffic. We coordinated with the British Nimrods and US Navy P-3s and sliced up the area of the water that we were searching so that we had good separation but you had stations for the fighters. There were tankers to worry about and the cab stations had to transit across what were still active airline routes at the time.

We flew into several of the other countries there in the coalition. We were members of the coalition and we could see the physical evidence of the build-up.

We coordinated with the other coalition members' squadrons and the training exercises. Training was intense at that time so we were flying from airwing or flying training sorties with the other coalition members and training with the US Air Force so there was intense training in air combat going on between the US Air Force, the US Navy and coalition air forces in preparation for what was to be Desert Storm.

So it's, I have to say, you know, that the other coalition member air force pilots I talked to were, their morale was high, they were anxious to train and they had new equipment and they were as anxious to train. And I think that they were very much anxious and thankful for the presence of the US Navy and the US Air Force there to assist them. I don't think that they were prepared to meet Saddam Hussein on their own.

The whole feeling at any time you went into one of these countries was that this guy was a madman, he was a threat to the area, he was not interested in peaceful coexistence in the area, he was interested in taking everything over and changing their life style and infringing on their national sovereignty so they were very much concerned about how to stop him and as I said before they didn't think that they could do it by themselves or they wouldn't have asked us there. And they were very thankful for us to be there.

We would be flying on these Iraqi ships and they carried small arms, we knew that, and they carried, they had the potential for carrying shoulder-held surface to air missiles, but the job had to be done so we would be flying at 200 feet off the water within hundreds of feet of these ships and all we could do was keep a sharp eye out and if we saw anything we would have to handle our speed to get out of the envelope with a weapon. So there was some concern, I won't say fear, but there was some concern. We were alert for it. And certainly as the boardings, as some of the boardings became more hostile than others, and we became more alert for anything that they might do as we were flying around them. We never saw anything pointed at us, but like I said we stayed alert for it.

It's good to be back.

RICHARD V. TORRES, JR.

Rank: Lance Corporal
Service: Marine Corp
Duty: Infantry
Hometown: Redlands, California

We got here the first of September. We left about six and a half months ago. And all we did was set up blocking positions the whole time out there until the offensive started. So the whole time we just moved around a lot and . . . we didn't always know where we were at. They told us names but the names didn't stick.

We were roughly about 800 meters away from a Cobra attack in the second line of defense that they had in Kuwait. And we handled close to 4,000 POWs. They were just like normal people. They just—a lot of them spoke English. A lot of them spoke broken up English. A lot of the officers did. A lot of the enlisted—they could understand us, but they didn't really want to admit that they could. But you'd tell them something in English and they'd understand you. A lot of them didn't have boots. They didn't have no socks.

They were hurting pretty bad. They didn't have no gear with them when they surrendered. They left everything back where they were at. They just walked over with their hat on. They had on plain green cammies. They were real weatherbeaten. They were real thin, real skinny. They looked like they hadn't eaten for a while.

We lived in—not a foxhole, we had fighting holes in the Marine Corps. A foxhole is something you hide in. There's two different kinds. You got a fighting one and you got a hasty fighting one. We dug hasty fighting ones because we weren't going to stay there too long. So you just dig it deep enough—maybe waist deep, where you can get down in it in case you get attacked by artillery or air strike or something, you can get down inside of it. Basically they make it a little wider then your body so you can get down in it. But you can still fight from it. But you can't get hit that easy with it. If you're standing in a defensive position then you making them a little more bigger to keep your ammo and your food and all that. But these were just hasties so it took maybe an hour to dig them.

I had a shower yesterday. But in Kuwait we didn't take them the whole time over there.

What stands out most in my mind is the happiness we seen on the way to the airport yesterday. All the Kuwaiti people and the Saudi people waving flags and giving us the victory signs. It's something that will stick with me that I was a part of something that freed Kuwait.

When we first went in I was scared. It was the middle of the night so we didn't know what to expect and none of the actual fighting had begun yet. We were one of the first units in without the ground war starting. So it was kind of scary because we didn't know what kind of support we had with us. So we went in—it was just our company—it was kind of scary then but after the fighting started and they started breeching everything, we felt more comfortable because they said it was going real well for us.

I thought I was well trained. I think if they would have tried to fight us they wouldn't have had a chance. We're a lot more high tech then they are. We have more—different tactics that we use and could have used against them. Especially in an open area like that.

We're out of Kay Bay, Hawaii. I'm going home. I'm going home to California, probably for about two weeks and then I'll start taking leave, just to get moved in.

CELESTE WARNER HEYMANN

Rank: Civilian
Service: USO
Duty: Tent City Manager
Hometown: Unknown

Well, it was very difficult in the beginning, because of the emotional strain and stress we had sending our forces down to the Gulf. We really didn't know where they were going and to what they were going. We just knew that it would have been very, very difficult to see a situation like we had during Vietnam. And I guess we have learned a great deal from the Vietnam era, that we cannot treat our forces like we had done then. And we were deeply ashamed, and we have tried to do it much better now, and showing them that we do stand behind them, if we can't go with them to fight beside them, to really be here for them, and make them as comfortable as possible for the short duration they are with us.

We were quite amazed how upbeat the groups were. Of course, they were coming into the tent, this is a large tent, some extremely tired, some of them irritable, some of them slightly ill from the long flight. But emotionally, going down to the Gulf, they were on an upbeat note. They were very positive. It was—often we were talking just about that the Lord will be with us, and from them, they would come to us and say we are so positive and we are so full of hope, we will be back soon. It was quite amazing, the positive key and the positive note which was involved in it.

The graffiti inside the tent was not supposed to happen, or outside the tent, either. I was pulling very many night shifts, and being a smoker, I requested that we have a covered smoking area in the tent. And so we had this little foyer made in front of the tent, and immediately put up a sign, please sign the walls, because of the very close recollection of the Berlin Wall, and being in the close proximity of Berlin and the Wall had come down so shortly before, we wanted to do something similar to the Berlin Wall. And the airbase being the home of the Berlin Airlift, we wanted to have something for posterity, to put at our visitors center once we built it. So we put a sign on the wall, and we put markers on the wall saying, please sign the wooden wall. Well, it didn't stay with the wooden walls. We now have graffiti throughout the entire tent, from ceiling to bottom, even all the covered spaces are full of graffiti. Our refrigerators have become places of graffiti, and we definitely are searching all avenues now to preserve this.

Through the tent, personally, I'd say I've seen somewhere around . . . 80,000, because my average day is somewhere around sixteen hours, seven days a week. We are extremely blessed by the quality of the force we have in. It's an average right now between fifty percent American, fifty percent German nationals. Some British, some French people are helping us, who live in our area. We have volunteers traveling 110 miles to come into a night shift, and then work 10-12 hours. Our present volunteer roster stands at 1,512 volunteers. We have an average of about 4,000 volunteer hours a month. And we have like key people who have been putting in extremely many hours, who have been absolutely a blessing to us.

The food is—85 percent of the food is being donated. The rest of it is being purchased by the USO. We have roughly 800 sleeping places around us. We have run out of sleeping places, and we had to put groups of about 550 in our gym. We finally built an extra tent for overflow traffic, so that we do not have to block up the USO tent with cots. We have had 180 cots in there at one time.

We have received thousands and thousands of pounds of care packages from the general public in the United States. It has been so gratifying to have received all this. The soldiers were coming to our place, which we call the halfway place from home, in either direction, either down to the Gulf or back to home. And the support we have received from the States and the thank-you letters we have received from fathers and mothers and relatives and wives for what we have been doing, is unbelievable. It has been so heartwarming. We have received thousands of cards, we can't even count them any more, little greeting cards and mail for any service member, which we then displayed in our tent. Actually, we ran out of space. We had to go time and time again, and the thank-you notes we have received from the families is—it's beautiful. It is all the things—and we didn't expect it, because for us, it was just so natural to do this. And our estimation is that we will be still here in October, in 1991.

I think every nation and every country has a small group of anti-whatever. It doesn't have to be a war. It can be airplane noise, it can be somebody cutting off the wrong tree at the right time, or the right tree at the wrong time. You have this anti-faction anywhere in the world. And our demonstrations have dwindled down a considerable amount. As we saw today, they are now carrying multi-colored balloons with them, and the nasty notes and nasty banners are no longer visible. And the atmosphere itself, thanks also to the level-headedness of our security force and the German police, the atmosphere has been on a good note. We have been able to talk to them. They disperse after awhile, and especially when it got very cold during the winter. *(Laughs.)* Definitely ninety percent of the German public was behind the United States and all the forces who have gone down.

Our German volunteers have all been screened. Unfortunately, we cannot do without that, for security reasons. But all our German volunteers in Tent City have been screened prior to them working with us, and so they are really pro-American. But the normal attitude of the general public in Germany is pro-American. And they said we—the Americans and everyone else averted something much more disastrous in the long run.

What sticks in my mind the most? Well, I think it was on the 16th of November, 1990. We had already serviced three full 747s. That means about 400 troops per flight. We had served a total of about four to five C5s and a 141, when we were alerted that we were getting in at least one more 747 aircraft, full with about 450 troops—when we found out we had one package of cookies left, on a Sunday evening at ten P.M. One of the volunteers, in my absence, called ASN, asked them to help us, to get a note out to the American public. And it was a football night, so we had a really wide audience. By the time that 747 touched the ground, the first donors of food were marching in from the other side of the tent. We serviced not only that flight, but two more flights that night. We had over a hundred phone calls asking us what we needed. We had 54 families and people coming in, bringing food. I celebrated Christmas early. I prayed a lot, I thanked a lot, and I cried a lot that night. But that is just about the most stirring moment in this entire time.

RODNEY T. CROWELL

Rank: Corporal
Service: Marine Corps
Duty: Infantry
Hometown: Kirkland, Washington

While Desert Shield started we were currently deployed in Okinawa and we came over here in mid-January, and so right when the bombing started I was stuck in Spain for three days until we got clearance to go in. Currently our unit had gone through a CAGS and we'd been through CAGS twice already. In Twenty-Nine Palms it's a desert training for a month, you go out there for a month in the desert to have training. And so, like I said, we were stuck in Spain and so I got to see pretty much the starting of the bombing as far as on CNN and stuff like that. Kind of knew what was going on as far as the other people that were already over there.

When we got in there we moved into the First Marine Division camp, got attached to the First Marine Division and we were there for approximately three days and we moved up north by Khafji and sewed in our positions in there. And then after that we just moved along with the Third Marines as far as the breach manoeuver. Our job was handling POWs and security. Every time we'd pick up POWs the first thing they would say was "Food. Water. Mister, please. Food, water." And they were in pretty bad shape for the most part. Most of them. At least the front line troops were.

As far as our guidelines, they told us that to treat them with high respect and to treat them according to the

Geneva Convention rules, which we did. So they were treated very well. In fact, they really didn't want to leave us when we dropped them off to the next handling unit.

There was one that did speak fairly good English, and we used him kind of as an interpreter. We also had a Syrian that was in our unit so he also interpreted for intelligence. I'm not sure exactly what type of questions they asked him or anything like that. They had AK-47s, RPGs, basic Soviet-type weapons for front-line troops. They pretty much just threw everything down. They had a very little, maybe ten shots at the most far back on them and then they'd drop their weapons. It wasn't much.

The first night that we moved up to our positions by Khafji, what we called the eight o'clock Charlie—which was the frogs that kept hitting close around eight o'clock every night—and the first night we were out there it hit over by the port which was about three miles away, but it sounded like it was just right outside our bunkers. So kind of the style there made you realize that you really are hearing more than you know flying in. You didn't see much until then so it became a reality at that time.

ROBIN K. LEE

Rank: Staff Sergeant
Service: Army
Duty: Infantry
Hometown: Fort Hood, Texas

Well, let's start with our first mission. Our first mission was Berm Buster II. It was to go forward and let the enemy know that we were going to start probing around a berm to the east. That way the First Armored Division could have a clear path in the west. We went up, they pulled up forward. We practiced a lot, the called it Berm Buster I. We actually used live ammo to blow Berm Buster I on a practice berm.

I got there on the 8th of October. Living conditions were what could be expected, you know. We had tents there for a while, and we had a couple of hot meals a day, MREs. I'm in a Bradley. It's a—it's for the infantry, what it's supposed to do, it's got a 25-millimeter gun and a TOW action, a TOW, so it can get the dismounts, the infantry, the fire support they need to put them up closer to the enemy.

The guys in Kuwait, when we—we went around to the west, and when we pushed up there, they said we pushed up so fast that they, you know, so I think everybody did that pretty, they moved fast. At night, we watched the bombing raids at night. We'd sit and get the PVS-7s out from this side of the berm, for like four weeks they were bombing them. We sat there and just watched it. It would be like a light show. You'd see rounds going up, rounds coming down, a big white light when they dropped the bombs. We watched MRLS fire from right beside us, and artillery on—you know, the MRLS on the one side and the artillery firing on the other.

We stayed pretty safe. Our sister element, one-five, had two vehicles got knocked out.

JOANN L. COCHRAN

Rank: Civilian
Service: USO
Duty: Volunteer
Home State: California

Our family's been coming up here to Tent City since actually November and we have seen very many of the 147,000 people that have come through here. And I think one thing that really has impresed us has been the quality of the young people. We have been in Christian youth ministry back in California for the last 15 years so we have been dealing with young people, both in structured situations and out on the streets. So we've seen all sorts of different types of young people back in the streets of California.

And to come here and see thousands of young people who have goals, who have identity, who have purpose in their lives has given us a different view of where this country might be going because we've worked with a lot of unstructured people in the past. And the quality, the clarity in the minds of some of the young people has been very good. And we've been impressed with both the reality of what they were doing and why they were doing it. On the one hand, they were willing to sacrifice their lives to go out into war. On the other hand, they had enough sense to be afraid. And so that was good. We liked the balance there that we saw that was reality.

We really were afraid when this thing started beefing up that too many of the kids had a TV mentality of what war was all about. And we have found in our communications with them, especially the ones that are down there now and have been writing to us all through this, that they seem to have a good reality operating in their life.

We had to really sit down and spend time with people because on the top they were just out front when you talked to them for a couple of minutes. They were, like, "Yeah! We're going to go down there and we're going to do our job and we're gung-ho!" But if we had the opportunity, and we did have a few that we were able to sit down and talk with, they were afraid of what was going to happen to them, they were afraid that they were unprepared to cope with some of the things.

They knew they had been militarily trained properly but they didn't know what it would really be like, if they were going to have to kill somebody. They didn't know what it would be like. And some of them were afraid. More often, they were afraid of the impact the whole war was going to have on their families, both the married people of course and even the singles. They were very worried about how worried their mothers were going to be.

I was born during World War II in California, outside of an Army installation. So that wasn't really home. As soon as my father went overseas, we went back to Ohio. My husband and I were both raised in Ohio and were married there and then left immediately the next week and have never lived there since. So we were 12 years going around the country, working in many different places when he was in the service. And then we've spent the last 15 years in central California. He worked at Fort Ord as a civilian. And we've been here since last July—about eight months.

We came up here in November. Actually, the first time

we came, our older children who are here with us had heard on the radio that they needed help in Tent City and they thought it would be just an exciting, patriotic thing to do to go up and encourage the people going down there. So we came thinking it was on a one-time basis. And once we got up here and saw the hundreds and thousands a day coming in and heading down to what even at that time appeared was going to be a war, it just kind of captured our hearts.

We've seen both sides of the corn on the veterans' issue, I think. We have seen people who are Vietnam veterans who are still active duty who have come in and received a healing—that finally America is honoring her military men and women who fight. And then for others, it has struck a note of bitterness in their heart. And several times I've talked with people who have expressed that bitterness, of "Why couldn't they have done this for us when we came back?" And the way I dealt with that question was that I am from that era also and we have friends—two in particular—with whom we have spent many, many nights up, seeing them through some of their hard times through the course of years. And America realizes that they made a big mistake. And isn't there a healing in the fact that America doesn't want to repeat that mistake, that they want to do better this time. And in every case where I've met someone who was bitter like that, when I've said that America wants to repent for what they did, that they want to make good for what they did, that they want to say they're sorry, then the best way they can do that is by giving the honor to these troops. Then the people are willing to accept that and not take it personally. They're willing to say okay. I mean, one fellow we had to see through around that question a couple of times and say, "What more could they do?

What more could America do but to say they're sorry and to do it right the next time around?"

We've also said too, "Don't you think that middle-aged America right now is the people who were the young people in Vietnam?" And many people decided when this whole conflict first began that they were not going to be stumbled by the politics of it, they were not going to be stumbled by the criticism that came out of Vietnam, often from people who didn't even know what they really were talking about. Like, I don't know that much about politics. I cannot intelligently critique whether the decisions being made are correct or not. But many people just hopped on the bandwagon: "We're going to be against this. We're going to criticize this." And I think that a lot of people, having seen that mistake made when they were young, are like we are and said that that mistake won't be made again, no matter whether there are political problems here or not. We are going to stand behind the individual men because they are not responsible for what's happening and we are not going to allow their hearts and minds to be damaged the way it happened 20 years ago.

I think it was two weeks before Christmas. A group of very young marines came through and they knew they were headed right to the front lines. And some of them especially were impressed with the fact that our entire family—my husband and I and our three children—were here working together. And it really touched them from the family aspect. And they asked us if we would write to them. So we have continued communications with some of these fellas. They are with the Second Marine Division and they have been down there on the front all this time and they have been in Kuwait City and now they've been told they're going to be there for months. And last week we received a phone call in the middle of the night and it was one of the fellas. And I believe that the story goes something like, they had trucked down quite a long distance through the desert into one of the cities so that they could use the telephone and call home. And everyone was making their phone calls and he had tried several times to call home and couldn't get through to his mother. And so he said, "I just couldn't leave town without talking to somebody outside of here on the telephone."

And we had sent our address in hopes that if any of these fellows are coming back through Germany on their way home that they would call us. And so he had our phone number for that reason and he said, "I pulled out that letter and said, 'Oh, I know someone I can call!'" And so he called us and chatted and told us all about the war because he couldn't get his mother. *[Laughs.]*

One of our family members up here is our 12-year-old son. And he's always been very interested in military things. He seems to have a bend in that direction. From the time he was two years old, he was listening to the David and Goliath stories and I think that this programmed him towards battle and ethics and this sort of thing. So he's been up here with the rest of our family putting in over 100 hours so far, sending people down to the Gulf. And it's been very interesting that he has spent a lot of time sitting around talking to adult men, some of them old enough to be his father or his grandfather, and has communicated with them and they have shared their life with them—how they got to this point and what some of their fears are of the war.

And I think one of the most amazing things was the first large planeload that came back from the Gulf. We were in here and this particular group had sat out in a sandstorm for 34 hours waiting for the transportation. It had rained for four hours. They were caked with mud. Many of them were unshaven. And it wasn't that they were undone; their packs were already in one location and they just could not get it together too much more than that. They had seen a lot of battle and they were very tired. A captain or a major—my son would know—sat down and shared what had happened to him the whole time he was down there with my son. And I think because of the way that he could listen to it—you know, not just "Yahoo! Tell me about how much you blew up," but a real human interest there in who the man was and how he felt about things—he shared the whole thing with him: his buddies getting killed and the whole thing. And my son was able to tell us about this on the way home— the man's whole story—and really had it in good perspective, for a 12-year-old. And we know that being up here and talking with people in that depth of real-life issues is going to have a real profound impact on his life also.

STEVE BROOKS

Rank: Lance Corporal
Service: Marine Corps
Duty: Reconnaissance
Hometown: San Antonio, Texas

I got over there about 16th or 17th of August and I participated in Desert Storm. I was First Reconnaissance Battalion. We're supposed to gather intelligence for First Marine Division and we do odds and ends whatever they need done we'll go ahead and do it, special mission.

Well, sir, well, I'll tell you what, it was very sandy but I hated it. We lived out there I guess for, when we first got there we moved into ports at the pier, came right off the plane, went into the ports for about ten days. From there we moved to a camp, there was Campsite 15 and it was kinda like little trailer homes almost you'd say. And we lived there for about two weeks and about two weeks to a month and from there we went out to the desert. The whole time we're doing patrols out in the desert and we come back to those places.

Out there it was more, I mean, almost everything's mobilized 'cause it's such a fast moving war. There's all armor stuff so we were doing mostly whatchucallit working Hum-Vs but we did do foot patrols too, but whenever we'd go out somewhere if it was for any extended amount of time most of the time it was in a Hum-V. And we lived out, we lived out there for a good while, I guess, about five or six months, going like I'd say like a month and a half without showers most of the time.

We dug, we have always dug holes, 'cause, you know, at first we thought the threat of enemy air would be bigger, you know, at least somewhat so everywhere we went we dug holes for SCUD alert. So anywhere we went out in the sand we'd dig, you know, about an eight-foot hole and live out of the hole most of the time.

We were out in the field, you know, we were out there. At that time we were doing foot patrols and we were out there, let's see, 20, 30 miles from the border, just doing foot patrols and getting ready to go into training and we heard it over the radio and everyone just, I mean, the whole next week we were all just sitting around the radio listening to, you know, what's going on.

We couldn't see the bombing. We could hear sometimes the bombing, but we saw planes going everywhere. I mean, especially at night, they'd all be lifting up.

We came up on a lot of them, but it was happening so fast, everything was happening so fast, that most of them were giving up and no one was, I mean, it was getting so bad that people were just bypassing these guys. They weren't even, you know, they weren't like a threat. Actually, they should have been treated as one, but it was happening so fast that people were passing them up, just trying to get up to the front lines to take care of everything and they were bypassing these guys.

They looked like Saudis actually. They were real dark complected, dark hair, most, almost all of them have mustaches or beards 'cause I think you know those countries' facial hair's supposed to be a mental thing, I guess.

Before we went actually, anyone went in, I guess, we were operating, reconnaissance marines were operating on the border the whole time in the poses, you know, they had Iraqi positions on the other side of the border, right there. Kuwait and Iraq. They had the border I guess where they had their guards, they had houses there. They were pretty nice, constructed out of concrete, real thick stuff and on the other side they had a place that looked just like it, I guess, they were the border patrol before it all ticked off. And we went up there about three months. This was about a month before the bombing started, three months before the ground war.

You could see the guys, I mean, you'd wave at them and they'd wave back there on the other side. That was about three months before anything started. You wave at these guys and they'd back at you. We stayed on the border. We were just patrolling up and down the border just to make sure there was no, nobody coming across like Iraqis. We were rotating in and out of there. After the air war started, after, I guess, a couple weeks after that, they started saying, "Hey, we're going to pull out recon 'cause they're too light in the armored and stick LAI up there because—"

So they, uh, they say, "We're going to put LAI up there since they have a little bit of armor and they can get out of there faster 'cause we got a suspicion that Iraq is going to be trying to grab American military personnel and get them as hostages, you know, POWs. So that night, we were getting ready to withdraw, we were going to withdraw the next day. And that night's when the Khafji incident went down and one of our, they're not from our battalion, they're from other reconnaissance, they were up, I mean, we all lived together on reconnaissance community and they're Alpha company, we're Charlie company, got captured in Khafji. Everyone was withdrawing as all that stuff was happening but they were pretty hairy there.

LAI was supposed to come up there and they were getting, um, I know a couple friendly fire cases, you probably heard that, and a lot of it's true, you know. Friendly fire thing. I know the guy that shot one of his own LAIs on that. You know, it wasn't on purpose, he thought it was a tank, but it actually wasn't. It was his own people.

Then I went into Kuwait City. Well, what happened that night was we had evacuated. LAI came up and manned the post after the Khafji incident went down. I guess about, uh, well like about 48 hours, two days. About that. That's about how long it was. After they got that secure we started going back up to the border again. And then five days before the ground war, guys from our outfit, I'm in Charlie company, but Alpha company, they had patrols going in. Six days before anyone ever entered Kuwait as in military, getting ready to go in, you know, the ground offensive. They went in and Ripper was the spearhead. They went in to the Ripper's AO, like they send, I think, three teams out and these guys went in and part of the thing is that they humped in like 20 miles or 20 klicks as it was and they found spots that were supposed to be breached and did a rip on it through econo-veno lanes that they had.

And from there on they used that, from what we heard Ripper really needed that whenever they brought it back it'd change the whole scheme of manoeuvers for the whole division. Task Force Ripper was supposed to go in and so it was a good operation, I'm not sure what the name of that was, but we were waiting on the border at this whole time.

Well, our mission was to go in and clear some bunkers that were bypassed by Ripper so we went in. We cleared bunkers, saw some dead guys laying around. That was kinda my first experiences, I guess you'd say, a combat veteran. And it was pretty, you know, different. All the guys were kinda looking forward to it 'cause they've always heard about that and so they were kinda looking forward to seeing stuff like this and we saw it and it really didn't strike me as that much until I think about it now and it's kinda, I don't know, I don't like to think about it, I guess, but it wasn't what I expected.

It looked like the whole place was on fire, I mean, every couple miles you could see a well head busted off and it was just on fire. I mean the whole thing. It looked like hell. That's what we always say, "It looks like hell." It actually did.

Everything was wrecked, everything was shambles and there were fighting holes everywhere. Tanks everywhere that they just abandoned and left behind BDPs, BDRMs, everything, they just abandoned it, left it behind, whenever the ground offensive came through, guys were giving up. I mean, all you could see was fires and abandoned tanks and BMPs.

Matter of fact, the smoke was so black during the day it looked like night time and it rained a couple times where we were out there and it would rain oil. It wasn't rain, it was oil, you know, whenever it was raining. We, everything was covered in oil and by that time we didn't care because we'd been out there so long without showers we were just, you know wanting to get things over with.

I just got in yesterday and came in, we stopped in Greece and Ireland, we had a good time at both those places. And then we stopped in Bangor, Maine, in the United States and we walked out and they had a band playing, the veterans were all there, the VFW. And, I mean, the whole place was lined with people, civilians everywhere. And they said, we came in about 9:30 in the morning their time, and they said that it's like that every time anyone comes home. I mean, they have people 24 hours just rotating in and out of that place, three o'clock in the morning. It was great. I, you know, that was great, it was like going to a big football game, you know, high school, except everybody was there, you know, and cheering you on.

America pulled together and finally said, "Hey, we're supporting our troops," and this is good, you know. Whether it would have been a bloody war or not, they all stuck behind us. And I thought that was great.

The coalition troops all worked with us, but we didn't really get to see them a lot. Brits worked with us, but we just reported our information back to the division and they take care of that. But we did get to see a lot of them and talk to them.

Everything worked pretty good. They were nice guys, you know, and nothing, we had no problems of any sort.

FAY E. PEACOCK

Rank: Unknown
Service: Army
Duty: Truck Driver
Hometown: Columbus, Montana

I'm originally from Columbus, Montana. I've been here since starting January. I'm an 88 MIC which is a truck driver by trade and I've more or less been in the admin part of it for the bus drivers that are here, keep the paperwork straight and they've cut down on drivers here in the last weeks so I'm technically earning my pay now that way instead of driving a truck.

Until they had me on shift now I was going home weekends, then my husband went to the field here the other day so I've just got every other day off really and try to go home when I can. Yesterday was my first run. Went to Wiesbaden Hospital and didn't really have a whole lot patients but there were a few psych patients who were, doctors weren't going to let us go until they had a medic on there from the hospital to watch. But they went ahead and let the medics take care of what they had to do, you know. And it was pretty subdued. And people were real quiet. I mean as soon as they got on the bus they were z'd out and it wasn't a bad trip.

I've only been in here a couple of times in the last few weeks, but the people I have seen been pretty quick, you know. Some of them had a look about well, you know, I want to get out of here now. You know, during the service they understand that this is supposed to happen at any time, you know, like me, I was called up to go and you know I didn't want to go.

When my commander asked me if I was, if there was any reason why I couldn't go and I said, "Oh, jeez, here it comes." And needless to say, I didn't want to go, but you know I was ready. It has been pretty relaxed here as far as my part. Many people come back but they figure bus drivers will be here for at least another four weeks.

I couldn't really say how many people have come through here in the last couple of weeks. There's been a couple hundred you know as far as casualties. And most of the people they've actually had direct flights from Saudi back to the States more or less, you know. The prisoners, the POWs came back they was more or less under guard so they didn't really come through here.

CLINTON A. GRAHAM

Rank: Lance Corporal
Service: Marine Corps
Duty: Logistics
Hometown: Gold Hill, Oregon

I didn't actually go to the desert. First day I was on board USS Okinawa, that's an amphibious ship. We were scheduled at the time after we left the Philippines we were going to Hong Kong and there were rumors that we were going to go, but nobody thought too much of it because we were over in the Philippines and the Gulf seemed like a long ways away so chances of us going were pretty slim, everybody thought. So we went to Hong Kong, had five days there for liberty. After we left Hong Kong we found out that we were going to the Gulf and that we had to stop again by the Philippines and get restocked on everything for the trip over.

My job on the Okinawa was, I was working in the S-4 shop, a logistics type thing. Logistics and basically I kept the machines running, kept everything up to par on the equipment and just basically maintenance management.

We had, we had watches on the ship, but we didn't, we weren't too concerned about mines this time even though we were in mine country. And we didn't start having look-outs until after the Tripoli and Princeton got hit with the mines. So then the further up to the Northern part of the Gulf we got the more tight security became. We had guys that were stationed at several different areas throughout the ship with 50 cals. and M-16s and then we started having people looking out for mines and things like that after the Tripoli and the Princeton.

Up to the point of finding out that Saddam Hussein had a deadline to abide by, the 15th, we all thought, well, you know, this guy didn't have too many marbles in his head to begin with when the war started. We doubted that he was going to be pulling out because he had such a mass of troops and armament built up. We didn't think he was going to do anything at all, just basically our feelings on it that, we thought that he was trying to bluff us so we were prepared to go in the 15th and do whatever had to be done. But I say again, nobody thought too much of it at the time because, you know, there were a lot of elements involved. A lot of things could happen.

When the air strikes were starting, that's when everything went from boredom to a lot of frantic, almost frantic, it was very busy on the ship after that. Everybody was getting prepared for, for anything that could possibly happen. And there was a lot of action going on. We couldn't see any of the bombing or strafing or any of the ships firing, but where we were at, you could get up on the flight deck and you could look around and you could see literally dozens of ships in the surrounding area. I mean it looked like a cargo port or some port of entry or something like that, but this was the ocean in the middle of the Persian Gulf and you couldn't see anything aside from the ships but water as far as the eye could see. And there were a few aircraft that flew over from time to time.

We practiced a lot with the general quarters for any cases of emergency that could happen. There was a lot of times where it, the zebra station where we had all our hatches secured on the ship. That means, zebra means water tight integrity and things like that where if you got hit the damage would be minimal and it wouldn't be allowed to spread because of all the precautions taken.

We had, we had a lot of frigates out there. We had a lot of merchant trawlers floating around, but they were watched very closely. We had a few of the L-CACs out floating around, that's Landing Craft Air Cushion, I believe. And what it does is it rides on the surface of air, and it can go from, immediately from the ocean to the land with no problem and it's used in amphibious assaults.

We'd been riding an emotional roller coaster on going home and then staying in the Gulf and then going home, staying in the Gulf. Then pretty soon everybody, everybody's beliefs were kinda shot after that 'cause, you know, things weren't certain.

I left the ship on emergency leave, and after I got home I watched the news closely. After I got back, I was watching CNN and watching what was going on and after I'd gotten back the ground war had started and I guess the ground war didn't last but just a few days. So I was pretty relieved. I couldn't say how everybody was on the ship but I can imagine they were a little joyous that it was all over with and that they were finally able to come home. As it is yet, they still haven't gotten back. They'll be back in ten days.

The worst was not knowing what's going to happen. I mean, you're there. You know what you got to do and you're ready to do it at any time. It's just the waiting. Stress levels were fairly high. I wouldn't say it's not being able to sleep. There was a lot of boredom on the ship, but even with all the boredom that was there, you know, you're still tense. There was a few skirmishes between people here and there. That's just their way of relieving stress, but all in all I think everybody on board the USS Okinawa worked real well together. Navy and Marine alike.

ROBERT W. WARD

Rank: Staff Sergeant
Service: Army
Duty: Tank Commander
Hometown: Fort Wayne, Indiana

I'm a tank commander. Basically, I control the whole tank. I have the driver who drives, and he takes instructions from me. I navigate directions, issue the fire commands, tell the loader what round to load, I identify each target. There's four guys. There's a gunner, a driver, and a loader that takes care of it. I was assigned to Bravo Company 1321, with the First Cavalry Division, and we deployed over in October of '90, and we set up in defensive positions and waited. And kind of, we were in a defend mission, to, you know, just to see what was going to happen. And about January 14th, we moved up to the berm up by Hafar-Batin. And we sat there and watched—covered the border for any insurgents who was coming across, and one of our missions to secure the KKMC, King Fahd's military center.

I'm in an M1A1. The M1A1 is the newest system that they have out. I was originally—we brought over the M1s, and in December we transitioned over to the M1A1s, which has the 120 millimeter smooth bore, and the NBC over-pressurization, Nuclear Biological Chemical defense system. It's got an added-on armor to it, and it's—you've got a great survivability rate, plus it's got some—the rounds that will penetrate what we had.

From the M1 to the M1A1 was pretty smooth. We had some people that had been on it, and we went through a transition—Fort Knox sent a bunch of people down to show us the new system. And we went there, and from there we went out and shot a gunnery, and everybody shot either superior or distinguished on it.

We went up on G-Day plus about eight hours. We went up through the Wadi al Batin, and made light contact with the Iraqi 12th Armored Division and shot up some of their bunkers. The tank units to our left and right shot up some Iraqi and took on some of their artillery.

We reached a bunch of minefields and they had laid the minefields—they had the obstacles put out in front of them. And we kind of surprised ourselves and wherever there's a wire obstacle it's probably a minefield. And we started looking real close, and the rain that had come across had kind of washed the dirt off—the sand off the top of them so they were kind of sticking out of the ground.

We had one of the tanks hit a mine, and it blew the number one and number two road wheels, the road wheel arms off, and we had to recover that vehicle. And in my platoon, the third platoon of Bravo Company. We had these mine plows, and so we went out and plowed the way up to—which basically what it does it it's kind of like a blade that digs into the ground, and it throws the mines off to the side. So we plowed the mines the whole way up to that, and we had an 88, which is a recovery vehicle, pull it out of the minefield.

You would have to basically run over it, and when it did come up out of the ground, it's like taking a pitchfork going through, and then the blade is curved so it would throw it outside of the track onto the high ground. It digs about twelve inches into the ground, I think. And it threw it off to the side, you know. My tank, we hit an anti-personnel mine, and there was no damage to the tank, we just continued to move. In fact, the tank that did hit a mine, it was back in operation the next morning. They replaced both road wheel arms. Our maintenance section was just fantastic. They came out and would work all night long to get the tanks that went down. And since we had the M1s, we had no major problems with them at all.

The Air Force went through and did just a bang-up job, they made, you know—the system worked real well with the combined arms of the Air Force and the Army's ground forces. And they made the job a lot easier. They weakened their resistance. And one of the First Cav's missions was to go up and do a feint up through the Wadi which made him think we were coming in there, because the British were off to our right, and we went up and made contact, which caused the Republican Guard to pull out of their positions and move down to attack us. And once they did that, the First Armored Division got the word that the deception issue was working. So they turned in to the side and caught them all out of their holes which really, you know, made our job easy, because once we made contact with them and held them, and they moved down with the other forces, the other units came across to hit them in the flank and in the rear and shot 'em up.

The Brits were off to our right. I mean, in our formation, I was on the inside of our brigade, on the left side of our brigade, and the Brits were over to our right side moving up, and they were taking—I think—I don't know what they really had for tanks, but the first impression when we received fire. We started shooting back. We'd always been told—you know, we do all this training, and with either lasers or a tank shoots wooden targets. They don't shoot back. And the first time that they shot back, it was kind of like, hey, this is for real! And it brought everything that we'd all trained for into the light, and we'd say, hey, this is for real, and somebody, you know, can get hurt out here. And the other thing would probably be the artillery. We'd been always trained that the artillery was devastating. We took artillery fire that was kind of like, they were shooting off to our left or our right, you know, it just—it didn't affect our mission, we just continued to move even though they were dropping artillery on us.

They had some air bursts going off, and it was bouncing over us. And our—the people in the battalion just continued to move, and we just continued to drive on. Once they give us a mission, we were just going to take that mission all the way and continue on. And the training that we received, when everything started, when they started shooting back and started getting artillery, just instinct took over of all the training we had, it just, you know, it just made the job easy, it controlled panic all around. So we—there was nobody panicking in the unit.

A company is fourteen tanks. And we're task-force organized, which means we have a company of infantry which have the Bradley, the M2 Infantry Fighting Vehicle and they have a crew that operates, plus a squad of nine infantry dismounts that go out. And there's three companies, there are fourteen vehicles in each of the tank companies, and there are Bradley companies attached to us, and we're used to working together.

Basically, the brigade commander comes down and gets the battalion commander, and he gets all the company commanders together, and they decide they're going to interpret the battalion's—or the brigade's plan. And then it comes to the CO, the commander, passes it down to our lieutenant, and all the tank commanders receive an operation order, and then we sit down and say, all right, this is our slice of the pie, this is how we're going to do it, the commander's intent, and analyze and kind of—if we have a lot of time, then we'll sand-table it and discuss all the missions.

With the way we moved so fast, we got what they called fragos, fragmentation orders, and they said, move here, and we would talk briefly in between and say, all right, this is our mission, we're going to do this, and we would execute that. And that's—the platoon that was in, we have been together since August of '88, and the lieutenant has been with us since December of last year, so we've been a very cohesive unit, and it took very little, because everybody knew exactly what was going to happen, you know, how each one was going to react. Usually the lieutenant is anywhere from six months to a year. He'd been with us about eighteen months. He was really inactivated from the Second Armored Division.

It made it a cohesive unit, because everybody—we had been together for so long, and you wanted to be there for your buddy, plus you also knew how he would feel, how he does things, and how we do things, the other wingman, and a platoon leader and his wingman and a platoon sergeant and his wingman, both mine—both wingmen have been together for an even longer period of time.

We move in a platoon and we bound, we go in a bounding overwatch. One section will move forward, and the other section will cover that, and then we always— we never break any slower than two tanks at a time. Basically like the Air Force does. It would kind of depend on the mission. If we were in a running gun battle, we would continue to defend and provide fire for that. Basically the tank would be—we'd all go to what we call ground, which is basically stop behind a defensive position and engage the target and sanitize the area and make sure it's clear, and then if the crew was completely injured and they couldn't do self-aid on each other. Each vehicle that we had had a combat life-saver that had gone through extensive medical training that we received from our medics, and so if he was injured then one of the tank's wingmen would come back to provide cover, and then while the maintenance group—excuse me, the medical personnel would come up and continue on, or if they were tied up with something else, the other two would give immediate aid.

They would make it—the maintenance chief would make that decision on the scene, he'd say, we can't fix this, or we hook the 88, the recovery vehicle, up to it, and tow it back into our the field motor pool. And then they would either—they would make the decision back there, or if it was something that could be fixed on the spot, like which happened out there in the field, and they could fix it on the spot and just continue the mission, and the tank would be picked up by the following unit, and then it would be as soon as we set some place, it would rejoin our battle force.

We moved out in January, out of our base camps, about the 4th or 5th, and the last time I talked to my wife was at the end of December. And we didn't get back to the phones from the entire time from January until the end of the war, and we came back, and I'm on emergency leave now, I've got to get back there and take care of some stuff. I've got a chance to get in touch with her. But the mail system was a little slow at times.

Well, once we moved out of our base camp and moved up to the berm, we lived on the vehicles themselves, in the rain, or whatever, we just would—we continued to pull what we called 25 percent security, one man away on the vehicles at all times. And we couldn't build a hootch because that would be a—what we call a hootch would be a tarp or something like that.

We had to be ready to go at immediate contact. Part of our mission was to defend certain sectors. If they would push down this way, we had to be able to move on it. So we basically just kind of soaked up a lot of rain during the period of time, and when it wasn't raining, we just kind of slept on the top of the tank. And we lived kind of like, the system was, if we got a moment's notice, we had like fifteen to twenty minutes, and everybody would just shove their bags in the racks and move out.

The planners that made this operation, I would hate to play chess with any of the people at the top. But they broke it down, they said, all right, the M1 can go five hours reasonably, you know, as a safe side, of getting fuel. So we would move every five hours. And we would stop. And they, our battalion had decided that there would be two fuel tankers that would carry 2500 gallons of fuel with them at all times. We had two of those per company and two cargo haulers that carried all our ammunition on it, extra ammunition, because if we got a contact, they would be right there. So every time we stopped, they would refuel.

It takes—we were just using—we were just living off the back tanks, you could go farther than that, we were just using the back tanks. And that holds about 250 gallons of fuel. And we could pump that in in about ten minutes. It just uses a nozzle, but they have a high idle where the pump—my guess is like—we probably pumped about 20, 25 gallons a minute using that, so it only takes about four or five minutes to fill the rear tank. And then they move on to the next vehicle. And once the entire company is filled, then they will take the fuel tanker back to the field train and drop them off, and then we would move, and they would catch up—continue moving and they would catch up with us, and we always had fuel wherever we stopped. If we ever got any contact, we had the ammo and the fuel with us, and they would just drop back.

The temperatures got up real warm during the summer time. And we have an overpressurization system that just kind of—you can control the temperature, but the engine has to be running on that. But with the M1A1 we didn't use it a lot of times, because that tank has a cooling suit. And you wear it underneath your uniform, and you plug it into the host and the overpressurization then blows cool air on you, keeps you cool. But the way they devised it, we thought up the plan when we attacked, it was cool enough with, when we had our suits on, we were comfortable, so we really didn't have that much need during an attack. But during the summer it got real warm and we had to use our time in the morning and the afternoon.

Luckily no chemicals happened, but with the training we've done, nobody really feared chemicals. We felt confident with our system and our training we had. There's always something in the back of your mind, if chemical was there—if you fight tank against tank, you can shoot back. With chemicals, it's something that you see and you can't fight back against, you just go, you know, into a protective mode. But we had all talked about it, yeah, it's something we don't want to deal with, but it's always on the back of your mind. But it really didn't play a big factor in a way. We were really kind of—we did extensive training in it and we had faith in our system and equipment.

We were told, and we had been following the news in

the newspaper and through the radio, that they'd issued a January 15th deadline. We had originally thought that, okay, we're going to go up here and we're going to make a show so that they can see that yes, we are for real. And then it came down to it, okay, we need to use force to get him out. And then we got the warning order that we were going to—that they were going to attack, and so everybody just got together and okay, we're going to go with it, the train, everybody maintain calm. They say all right, let's just get it on so we can go home.

On the morning of the 15th it was kind of—we were sitting back, we had not moved up to the border yet. We were sitting behind Hafar al Batin I guess it was. And the CO came across the radio, and the guy who was on radio watch says, hey, the CO's got a message for us. And it was a warning order, and all of a sudden you saw all these planes flying overhead and the sky is lighting up and the lights going off, and it's like, hey, this is really going to happen, we're going to kick off, and we really thought that we were going to get involved that day. And we got the warning order to move up, and we moved up close to the berm at that time, and we were really, you know, we were really pumped.

And the artillery going off on the border. We were using our night sight. And it would light up, and you could watch the big flash and the burning and stuff, and it was an amazing display the Air Force put on. It was—it would make the Fourth of July look like it was, you know—a little firecracker.

They'd fly overhead, and go in through, and especially at night when the A-10s were dropping in, they dropped flares, and then they would light up the area, pick out a target, and you could watch the missiles fire off and take out the target, you'd see a big flash. Even in a 64-ton vehicle, it shakes every time one of those big bombs drops, and it was—after awhile, it was kind of like—you know, the first couple of days, it was everybody staying awake and watching what was going on. And then it kind of got, okay, I've seen enough of this. And it just—we got back into our normal routine. And then they started shooting the MLRS, the Morning Launch Rocket System, and to watch one of those go off, that's just an awesome display of firepower.

We didn't see any mobile SCUDs. We came across a bunch of damaged T-72s and BMT's. They're equivalent to our Bradley. And a bunch of other destroyed trucks and compounds and ammo bunkers. Some of the A-10s that we came across were either the Third or the First Armored Division came through, and shot armor piercing rounds through T-72s and just blew the turrets off the tanks. The rounds for the 120-millimeter on the M1s are just awesome.

We had a real good briefing before we came over here on T-72s. They brought a team around, and they climbed into it. I was impressed with the way the T-72, how it worked and the systems it had on it, but I—they said this is what its capabilities are. It's awful cramped inside, and they don't have the sophistication that the M1 has in survivability. We knew, you know, an M1 takes a lot of ammo compartmentwise, and if it gets hit back by the ammo, it will blow out the back where it won't damage the crew. And it's only got a certain area that you've got to worry in the tank, and we've got so much armor on the front, that we were really safe inside the tank. I told my crew that it's about 95, 95 percent survivability if we took a strike.

The M1—we went from—we pulled to the Wadi to do the feint mission, and we pulled from back there, and then followed the First Infantry Division, the First AD, the First Armored Division, the Third Armored Division, followed them up through the breach that they had made and made contact, and we made—it was referred to when Patton made his relief about Somme, we travelled farther and faster than he did. And we didn't lose a vehicle, and we ride with fourteen tanks and every Bradley we took up there we arrived there with. We had a super maintenance program, the maintenance people we had were just awesome.

We'd get an operations order, and we would execute it. Everybody knew what was going on, commanders knew what was going on. And even when we got the frago to change the mission, that we were going to do this, we had enough information that we could everybody knew what was going on, the commander briefed the lieutenants, the lieutenants came down to our platoons and briefed all the tank commanders when the time had come. It was short notice, frago gives you basically a little short notice, like here's what's going to happen. And our training just took over from there. And the way they had this orchestrated from above, with his plans and the way everything was figured in, because we got the briefing laid out, and they said, this is going to be here, this is going to be here, once we've moved to this point, these units will move up. They had it all broke down all the way up, everybody knew what was going to happen from the lowest guy to the highest guy.

And then a tank commander briefs his crew on what was going on in case something happens to him. And so the whole crew knew what was going on, and everybody was very comfortable and talking about what was going on.

We were getting ready to attack when the cease-fire

was announced. We started moving and we got held in place, and we got some reports of vehicles moving around another area so we reacted to those. And we spent about two days at a higher recon level just outside the area. And finally they said, okay, fine, we're stopping here. We were close to Basra. We stopped there and maintained a posture, and as things calmed down, we got pulled out about five days ago out of our deployment to rest and recuperate.

The saddest part of the whole war, was to see the condition of the Iraqi soldiers. They were weak, they were—if we would have, you know, mistreated them or rough-handled them in any way, you almost had to think that they would just break in your hand. They had no food. They had a small jug of water with them. Their equipment was rusty. They were just trying to make it back when we ran across them. And they just surrendered. And we said, okay, we took great care of them, we gave them food and water. The first sergeant came up and took care of them, searched them, and they were just "Thank you, thank you."

And I talked to several guys from other units that they ran across and they were just, "Thank you, mister, thank you, mister." And they were so weak that they couldn't even open our meals, our meals-ready-to-eat that we have, they couldn't open those. They had regular uniforms on and winter coats, but one of the guys we came across had no shoes. He had socks on, I don't know how they kept warm or he was trying to walk, but some of them were just—they mostly have warm clothing, but some of them didn't.

It was kind of, just kind of depends on what units you ran across. But they were—it was just a shame to see them, you felt so sorry for them. I don't think there's no way that any Americans could have rough-treated them, because they were just even the guys who were in the front and exposed in the immediate—you felt so sorry for them, that was one of the major problems, is we would run across major areas of POWs, and it would slow the flow of momentum down. So finally we had to just give them water, take the weapons and say, all right, there's somebody coming along, just stay here. And somebody would pick them up. And it would basically slow the whole momentum down.

We took all their weapons away from them, and did a quick search on them and give them food and water, and once that happens, they were—a guy who was on a work team came across and he asked, "Are you going to kill us?" And we said, "No, we're not going to kill you, we're going to feed you and give you water." "Thank you, mister, thank you, mister." Oh, just, we were the greatest, and stuff.

They were told that we would kill them, violate them, mistreat them, torture them, and all of this was going on, and that was the farthest thing—we were told from the very git-go how to handle POWs, and that was even before we deployed over here. How to treat soldiers, because of all the stories of what happened during World War II with our mistreating, and it made the units fight harder. We took great care of them, but they were told they were going to be killed, we were going to torture and violate them, just mutilate them. And I talked to several people who had gone back to the other area before the ground war, and they were basically, you know, they couldn't believe that we were allowing them to practice religion. We let them do their religion and fed them, and they were just amazed at how well they were being treated.

When we'd mention Saddam Hussein, a lot of them made a gesture of cutting their throat. One of them that we captured called him a donkey. And they just would spit on the ground every time you mentioned his name. We ran through a couple of Republican Guards, but they were basically, they were not as well trained a Republican Guard, they just kind of—in fact, one of them said that—a friend of mine is in an alert team, and he came across this, this guy walks out and says, we would have surrendered days ago but you were too far away to walk. So they waited until they got close and they walked out with 200 people on line. And they gave them no problem, they would do anything that you said. And they were offering them their money. One of them was searched, and had what would be a grenade, he thought, and he pulled it out and it was a hard piece of bread. And the guy insisted that the guy take it, he said, no, you need that, in fact, here, have an MRE to eat. And the guy ate it and, "Oh, thank you, mister." They were giving them money, anything that they had in their possession, to give to the guys.

The problems before we ran into, a couple of times was, a group would want to surrender, but a certain group wouldn't. So they would put up a fight while they were going on, but a lot of the other units were reporting that they would shoot a magazine of their AK-47s, and as soon as that went off, they just raised their hands and surrendered. Kind of like they were just putting up token resistance to let them know, you know, for their orders, I guess, their officers. They were told that—the officers were being held accountable for anybody that deserted from their unit.

And they would be executed if they found them like listening to Voice of America, or reading propaganda from our side, they would just execute them on the spot. Or if they tried to escape. We expected—we dropped these leaflets, that I've got, I picked up a couple, that told them, you know, if you do the following conditions, you will not die. And that kind of became an incident after Khafji. Because they came in and they were going to surrender, and then all of a sudden they turned the guns around.

They just opened up on them, that's the report we got. We weren't close to that area. So that made us think, you know, wait a minute, is the same thing going to happen to us? But they would just hold their hands up and throw their weapons down so they would never, you know, just—they didn't want no tangling with tanks and the M1s. And they had watched several of their tanks I guess just get blown out from underneath them, or around them in areas, with the M1s. And I don't know how many M1s that we lost over here, but it was very, very few. We took out the fourth largest army in 100 hours.

The Air Force took out a lot, weakened them up, which made our job easier. It was just like a sort of combined team fighting, and the guys at the top, the generals, really knew what they doing.

I was talking to some guys who set up the first . . . division again and they said that they had gotten a report that a medivac had flown in. I asked them what was going on and they said that one of the POW's was so scared and didn't get searched and he was wounded and a doctor came over to help him out to treat him and the Iraqi POW was scared, didn't know what was going on and thought we were going to torture him, as was told to him before. And he drew his gun out and shot the doctor and killed him.

I think it was just more fear from the unknown, being

told what was going to happen, you know. Just talking to other people, they said that the marines would skin them alive, that we would torture them, that we would eat them, one of the other stories we heard said that we would violate them, we would torture them, kill them on sight, not let them practice religion which was all just a lie because like I said before, they practiced religion, we fed them, took good care of them. A lot of them just wanted to stay on our side and didn't want to go home.

I'm still kind of riding an emotional high that we did a good job and everything came out okay. I brought my entire—everybody in my company—is coming back alive. We all thought we did a good job. The inner service, working together, is pretty good. I'm not really having nightmares like you know, they experienced during Vietnam, but you know, with all the artillery fire, I've kind of become accustomed to hearing it. I don't know how it's going to be in several months if I hear—like the 4th of July, or something like that—but I don't feel it's going to be a problem.

In fact, when it first started, I had called another tank commander and said these guys are shooting back and it was kind of like, you could feel the tension come across you. You could feel the emotion that "Hey, this is for real, it's no longer a training exercise." Because your first—what they call blooding, I guess—when you go against an enemy, you don't know how to react. And it was kind of like, "Okay, this is like the instruction, the drill that we did." That took over right then, and it was just like you know, let's get down to business and let's just continue on.

With all the units on the line, we were starting—we just got our operations orders to put all the divisions on line and we're just going to continue to drive into Kuwait, eliminating anything they had. All isolated pockets of resistance they had. By the time that we had come down to them there were just isolated pockets of different brigades of the Republican Guard still floating around and with the intercooperation with the services, the Apaches were spotting targets, tanks were firing on it, the Apaches were firing on it, the alert teams were out in front, the reconnaissance patrol—they were out there spotting the targets and saying, "Hey, just clear up to this point." The helicopters were flying up and hitting the targets. The tanks were moving and bounding forward. It was an awesome display of firepower. And not everybody got a chance to shoot because everybody did their jobs. It's just like some guys kind of just rode along, because there were just not a lot of targets to shoot at.

M.J. HOLMES

Rank: Private First Class
Service: Marine Corps
Duty: Mechanic
Home State: Arizona

I was working for the sheriff department down in Arizona, and I was also going to school at the time attending night classes for computer repair when I got orders to report to Camp Pendleton. I was out since 1984. It's been a long time. The Marine Corps has really changed a lot for me so it's really a little hard getting back into things but eventually I'll get back into it. I guess because of the war starting I was reactivated. After seven years, I really don't now why, but they recalled me and I just got orders and I went with my orders, whatever.

I have a family, but I left them behind to be here. But I call 'em every three or four days to let 'em know that I was still here at Camp Pendleton and I didn't get to go. They're more happy just hearing the war being over than I was not going to be there. But I got a two-year hitch with the Corps now so they're going to be here for two years before I even go back to see my family.

They left my job open. They figure as soon as I get back I have about 90 days notice to report back to the sheriff department and keep the same experience or whatever you want to call it that I have with them.

I just reported here to Camp Pendleton main side and I guess I was always ready to go in a moment's notice. I was ready to go. I would have been basically in the main COC area, just laying wires of different length, setting up communications. Far as like movement, I probably wouldn't even be moving as much as radio operators would have been. So I would have been, because of all the wire we would have to lay and pick up and leave so that's about what a wireman does. Unless he is up with a line company. If he's up with a line company then he's gonna be out with the grunts. He's gonna be out there. That's what I was before with the line company and during my training at that time we moved a lot. We set up and broke down and set up a lot of times, in a couple of days we set up six, seven times.

SILVANO J. ZOBELE

Rank: Staff Sergeant
Service: Air Force
Duty: Aerial Port Coordination
Hometown: Bronx, New York

I worked for Metropolitan Life Insurance Company, as a computer programmer, at the home office in New York City. And I was activated the 16th of December, 1990. And for the first three months, I worked at McGuire Air Force Base as an aerial port person, basically responsible for movements of people, cargo, in support of Desert Shield and Desert Storm.

Well, unlike some other people, probably a lot of people, I was fortunate in the sense that I'm not married, I have a job that is pretty liberal in the sense that they gave me no problems. They are paying part of my salary while I'm on active duty. Making up the difference between the Air Force, like the Air Force base pay and regular pay. And in the company I work for, I think there's about maybe a dozen people throughout the company of almost thirty thousand people that are involved in this operation. So it's not a big problem for the company. It's not like they've lost a hundred people. So it's pretty easy for the company. And unlike other people, I have no debts or problems, so it wasn't much of a hardship, other than my home, which is in New York City, because basically no one's living there right now, but I'm having somebody look in on the house. So I've been fortunate that I haven't had any problems.

I've heard from—I've heard, you know, from other

people, that some people are very happy, in support of Desert Storm, and other people are not so happy. Some people say as soon as this is all over, they're getting out. Getting out of the reserves, they're not re-enlisting. How true that is, whether they're just upset at the moment, I'm not sure, but I would imagine some of the people who have less time in the service may re-think their participation in the program. They may not sign up again.

We expected that we probably would go over. So we were not surprised. We were briefed on conditions there and the length of stay.

RICHARD O. MOORE III

Rank: Lance Corporal
Service: Marine Corps
Duty: Infantry
Hometown: Wooster, Massachusetts

I'm 20 years old, I'm from Wooster, Massachusetts. I'm an infantry man, small gunner. Basically what it was like out there was we got here in September and we had a lot of training for different missions we were coming up with for the upcoming war and a lot of things changed while we were there. You know, we had various missions, depending on what we were going to do and how the Iraqis did their movements and everything. And from there on we moved around a lot in the desert, we came up to a lot of places.

At the start of the war we were the first battalion in. We were two days ahead of Task Force Ripper and Task Force Papa Bear. We set in and we got fired upon by mortars. We didn't take any casualties, we breached three mine fields—you've got three different kinds—you've got a deliberate breach, a hasty breach and then an assault breach, okay? And what that is is being that we're grunts, we have to carry portable line chargers with us, so we just bar them off, we probe up to the mine fields—you know you check the mines—and from there on, you know, you're just on your own from there.

Their mines are sophisticated. They're plastics—my second MOS is demolitions so I do a lot of blowing up the mines in my job and the ones they have are sophisticated. They're all plastic, they have very integrated mechanisms to start them off with. It takes a varying amount of light pressure to set them off. They have pretty good antipersonnel mines and anti-tank mines. But what they did wrong was they had left them above the deck so we could see most of them. And what we had done, we had reconnaissance battalions go up there and you know, break out a fucking plan—excuse me, break out a plan—for me, for us, and then we assaulted on through.

Their morale was pretty low. They had no uniforms, no uniformity at all. They all had different colored uniforms on, different gear and stuff like that, whereas if you look at the Marine Corps, everything's just perfect, you know, so you could distinguish between each other. Their's were unlike that. They were pretty happy to be caught, you know, actually. Because we couldn't handle so many of them, we just had to let them keep walking south until some administration battalions picked them up and then you know, we'd just get the credit for them.

I was at Khafji. What happened was that they came across—Khafji is about fifty miles from the border. And in between there it is a holding place for tanks—you know mine tank traps and things like that—so they had turned their turrets around and they did everything that these little pamphlets said they were supposed to do, I don't know if you've seen any of them. You see, we had our artillery battalion fire these things out—they're called bomblets—and they show here you know, the Iraqis getting shot and giving up and you'd be going back home to your family and so on—in Arabic and in English. So they applied by these conventions here and they came across, they just turned their guns around and opened fire on the marines who were there.

It was a real downer, you know. That's it. I seen—when I did the breach, I seen—B52s carpet bomb the area that we came through. Well, that was incredible. I mean there's no feeling like it, you know, it's like getting—kind of being in an earthquake, everything shaking—worse, it feels worse, except that the ground's not opening up on you. Khafji—Khafji's a mess. The whole town's a mess. We did a lot of house-to-house clearing to clean the Iraqis out and you know, everything was pretty raked. They took everything.

GLENN JOSEPH SADOWSKI

Rank: Second Lieutenant
Service: Marine Corps
Duty: Light Armor Infantry
Hometown: Yonkers, New York

I left the U.S. August 16th and we arrived in Saudi Arabia late, early on the morning of the 18th. I was platoon commander for light armored infantry platoon. We had the LAV, the light armored vehicle. LAV-25. It's a good vehicle. It's an 8-wheeled vehicle.

As platoon commander, my responsibility is the tactical employment of my platoon. We were—Attack Force Shepherd was the battalion of light armored vehicles—when you have a big mechanized one like that a good portion of the light armored vehicles plunge forward 'cause we have so much speed and pretty good fire power for a vehicle that size. To plunge forward and locate the enemy and report back to the heavy mech battalions that are coming up our rear, just give them information so they could properly deploy their units to meet the enemy threat coming on. So we were always up on the front.

The night of the 29th when we came over and took Khafji, my company was sitting out by Al-Mejal. We were right there directly involved with that battle. My company of LAVs with two attachments stopped a battalion of enemy tanks in a mech battalion. Just a company of LAVs.

A LAV company's made up of two LAV platoons, six vehicles each, so that's—plus the headquarters 25, that's about 13 25s, along with two vehicles of recovery, that's about 15. Total vehicles we had about 20-something vehicles, light armored vehicles as compared to a battalion of about 50 tanks and 50 VMPs and VIDMs. And they all tried to come across the border that night. We stopped them. We stopped them with our direct fire from TOWs.

They're LAV but they have TOW missiles, hammer shoot two TOW missiles but only one at a time. Well, we deployed them. We stopped them coming through because there was a big choke point. Just by our fire. We didn't hit anything 'cause it was night. We opened up on them and got involved in a fire fight, gave us time to get air on station, then we pulled back, sat on line, took them out with air, just stopped them cold. Till we had to pull back, one of our vehicles got hit by, uh, friendly fire. From the air. That was the biggest problem in the whole war was friendly fire.

It happened everywhere. I mean everywhere there's shooting 'cause they was so many men and such a little space pushing through. It was just so hard to coordinate. We weren't in Khafji. They tried, they pushed through the border in three spots. One was at Khafji, Khafji was abandoned so they moved right into it, it was not even a fight for it except the retaking.

Then they came in another spot, just drove along and went back up and then they came in at Al-Mejal. And that's where my company was. And on the same night those 11 marines that were reported killed at Khafji were killed at our battle. They weren't killed at Khafji. That vehicle that blew up was my wingman. About 100 meters to my right. A maverick from a A-10 hit him, that's what we believe it was.

I came over here, the day I, I got out of TPS, took 30 days leave, I came in here and I was checking in my unit here at Pendleton. The day I checked in they were called upon to put 300 volunteers to go over to Saudi Arabia, 300 enlisted and five lieutenants and I checked in and the colonel wasn't there, the battalion ExO, came up and said, "Hey, this is, lieutenant, this is a great career opportunity. You want to go to Saudi Arabia?" And I'm probably, I figured I was better prepared than anyone else 'cause I was fresh out of school. I had everything in my mind. And at this point I'm thinking I'm going to be a rifle platoon commander. All, all the newest things, you know, the newest tactics came out of IOC and I just learned them so I said, "Sure, I'll go." And it turned out I got LAVs just by the stroke of the pen 'cause usually that's a job for a senior first lieutenant. I'm a boot second lieutenant. So I got it. I really didn't have any, it's a secondary MOS, you go to school for it.

I did on-the-job training and I tell you the first couple months in Desert Shield I was just flailing around, but I picked it up and by the time it got time to do the job I did it just as good as any other first lieutenant if not better. The colonel said he wants to keep me. I'll do it 'cause I can't go back to the grunts.

When the bombing started, we were in a position with Task Force Ripper, screening for Ripper. And, uh, I just remember my fire watch and the company came over the radio and our fire watch came over and woke me up and said, "They started bombing."

I woke up and at that point we had 24-hour LPOPs and our positions of guys looking out up to the north or the west, wherever, a flank, just to make sure nothing was coming down our way. He figured he might have an attack so I walked up to see how my OP was doing, you know, and tell him the news 'cause they didn't have a radio up there that was on company tac. And I walked up and told him and we saw a light off in the distance. I said, "Hey, you know, it's light," and it was pretty far away, 30 klicks.

It just looked like a light, it looked like something burning 'cause it was expanding and getting smaller. And I said well, that might have been there for a while and it turned out that it was a truck column, just pickup trucks with their lights on coming back.

And it got closer. It was Saudi Arabian military police. They got closer and I had only two vehicles there. I was covering a 10 klick frontage. I was covering this section with two LAV-25s and two HumV TOW vehicles. And that's all that was at this position, you know, and these 30 trucks come screaming down, Saudi military police with 50 cals and 12 sevens on the back. And it must have been about 30 trucks. And I had two guys on OP and the AT jumped out and stopped them and he wanted to know what the hell they were doing and they said they had to get back somewhere. They were all scared, pissing in their pants. And a sergeant was up there, he's going, "Lieutenant, these guys are running scared, they're running scared."

If they've got to run, I can't stop them. I'm not their lieutenant, so I called my CO and said will you authorize our vehicles to escort them through our lines to let them go and hope nothing was coming for them. They just said they saw the explosions and ran scared. And we just sat there waiting for anything to happen and nothing happened, nothing came down.

We weren't up that close. We didn't get up that close till the night of the 29th. We set in that position hours before they came across. Just set in. What spotted them first was, there was tracer fire, a recon unit started calling all these tanks coming down. We had a battalion recon unit on the other side. They called all these tanks coming down, retreated before this building and started having a fire fight with tanks, grunts, guys with 203s and SAWs and AT-4s and taking on tanks when they should have been running.

And then they called us up for help but what woke us up immediately was they had all this small arms fire going and one of my radio watches woke me up and said, "We got small arms fire." And before they said it, you know, when you're up on the border you see that stuff all the time. And I told him, "You see that stuff all the time." And he said, "No, lieutenant, this is closer."

I didn't want it to be another Beirut, so we always kept our guard up even to Desert Shield. Everything was so lax, and I always wanted to make sure we kept a guard in a good state of alertness. I had six light armored vehicles and a minimum of 42 marines. It fluctuated up to 48 at times. In the vehicles during the battles I didn't know what was going on on the other vehicles. I had to rely heavily on the vehicle commander, the commander of that vehicle which each commander was a sergeant.

I was directly responsible for my vehicle and I only had a slight problem with one guy who was a little bit shaky. But I had other problems on other vehicles. After the battle the VCs came up to me and said this guy, you know, was kind of, well, how do you put it? He spazzed out. And there was two others and we put them in the H&S platoon which was with us but kept behind us. That's Headquarters and Supply. So we stuck them with our log vehicles so they were kept behind us. We were a line company, but they would be behind the line platoons. They wouldn't be directly in fire, but they would be called up to be under fire.

I don't think those few guys deserved to be in the

Marine Corps. I'm not being a hardass or anything, I'm far from that, but that's ridiculous if a . . . that's a primary job and if they can't do it, what the hell are they doing here? Why are they drawing a paycheck if they can't do what they're called upon to do?

It was under fire, but all I'm asking is just stay calm. I mean, some guys can't do it and they, these guys who did spaz out, I mean, there's no way—I thought so highly of them before that. All these guys could bench press a car, they were consistent 300 PFTers. Hard working, motivated, all the time. And you figure some shitbird would buckle. When it happened to a couple of them , the VCs told me, I said I couldn't believe it, but after that, you now, they couldn't do their job. They're not marines to me anymore. If they can't do that, every guy who pushes a pencil in the headquarters office has got to be able to take up a rifle and fight for us. That's our job.

One guy was telling me, I mean, I'm not a psychiatrist, but he's like, "Oh, I feel depressed every day. I'm waking up with all this foreboding." He was trying to say about the other vehicle getting hit and I said—I don't want to use his name—I said, "Look, uh, what's your problem? You scared?" And he said, "Yeah, I'm scared."

I go, "All right, I don't want you in my platoon. I'm going to do my best to get you out of here, but as far as I'm concerned you're a piece of shit. And I'll get you into A-Corps and get another man." But I said, "If we were back in the States I'd do everything I could to get you out of the Marine Corps 'cause you don't belong in here."

The next day when we were back there was POWs. We had hit some tanks with our HE rounds and from 25s, they cannot, they can't penetrate the armor of a tank. The HE rounds like a grenade and we can put that out pretty far, farther than I expected. We had these tanks, we were out of their range, but we could hit them. And when we talked to POWs they said we were hitting the vision blocks on the tanks 'cause they were all buttoned up and they couldn't see so they got out of the tanks, ran into OP-4, left the tanks and the air came in and blew them up. And they just gave up the next day.

I seen it happen. When we going through Kuwait, we were attached with Ripper and they made no qualms about it. If there was a tank out there, abandoned or not, they took it out. They weren't taking any chances. And that's the way you got to do it.

It was like the country was burning. 'Cause there was oil fires everywhere and it got so bad that it was like driving into the thickest fire you could ever see and you couldn't see 50 meters, you couldn't see a vehicle 50 meters to your left or right. I don't know if it was a strategic move on his part, I think he just did it to kind of spite us, but it was a good strategic move on Hussein's part to do that 'cause we couldn't call in air and we were floundering around in the fog. And if he had stayed and fought, it would have been a different story. It would have been us rolling up on guys sitting in a defense with engines shut down. They could have heard us coming and you couldn't see. You were ready to rely on hearing. They'd know we were coming. They could have taken us out pretty bad.

We didn't have no trouble breathing. We didn't feel it. I'm sure I inhaled a lot of smoke but you couldn't feel it. But you just got dirt all over you. I didn't sleep much but I didn't really have to. First night we went in late I got about an hour's sleep. When I slept sitting up in the VC's hatch. The second night I got about four hours.

When you go through, now they don't do it, but back in OCS we got about for six weeks we got about five hours sleep a night and did some of the most physical training I've ever done in my Marine Corps history that's like our boot camp for officers. So now they make sure you get eight hours 'cause some bleeding heart liberal said it was too cruel, but this is what officers got to be trained for 'cause we got to do what we got to do. We got to be everywhere and doing everything when the battle comes. It's our responsibility. I would walk the lines checking all my vehicles at night and we'd be spread out like a klick, you know, just from moral support for the men and to see whether the VC had anything for me and this called for me to be awake a lot. And at TBS they kept us awake and out in the field doing a tactical problem, we were awake all the time.

We had mechanics with us in our recovery vehicle for the company. And we didn't have any problems during the whole Kuwait war. When we first got there, the vehicles came off the MPF ship. You know, they had been sitting in storage and we had mechanical problems with them then during Desert Shield. You know, just because they had been running and they hadn't been for a while. And then, it was consistent problems with all the LAVs. It was exhaust problems, then some belts, but as we kept using them and breaking them in, and replacing them with new parts, we knew what to do and by the time we were rolling in for Operation Desert Storm our vehicles were good to go and we had no problems with them during all of Operation Desert Storm.

They run on diesel fuel, we were using JP-5 and JP-8. They can burn any of it. That's what caused our exhaust problem, we were using JP-5 and JP-8 . . . that's plane fuel . . . and it burned our exhaust hot, got some holes in it. We always carried our own fuel with us and with our log train, that was part of our log train, we had a fuel truck with us so there was no problem, but it didn't last that long. It never got to where it was so spread out. I mean, when we was attached to Ripper there was a huge, they call it a combat train, like a log train. And they always had all the fuel and ammo you could want.

I was so pumped up. We pulled back when our vehicle got hit by air 'cause it was a burning hulk and where my platoon was it was outlining everybody so we were marked for the enemy so we pulled back and switched lines with another company. They came up 'cause we had been fighting that battle for four hours. And I tell you the truth it seemed like I was doing it for 15 minutes.

We pulled back and another unit pulled up and we went back immediately, refueled, rearmed and in the morning we flipflopped again. If they kept going it would have been trouble. We were outnumbered and our vehicles weren't made to take out a tank. If they were marines, we would have been in trouble. Their equipment wasn't bad. It was the people using it.

I didn't really talk to many prisoners. 'Cause we were moving so fast we disarmed them and sent them back to the guys who were going to handle them. They all seemed like, I mean, they gave up willingly enough but I heard rumors, I never heard from an Iraqi himself, but I heard rumors that they always thought marines had to kill their parents to get in the Marine Corps and this and that and I've heard other countries hear tales of us being a bunch of animals, but I guess it's just a reputation. It's good to have when you go into battle.

MICHAEL J. KEMMER

Rank: Lieutenant Colonel
Service: Air Force
Duty: Electronic Combat Planning
Home State: Pennsylvania

Basically what happened was Brigadier General Henry was forming an electronic combat cell down there and said, "Hey, we need some expertise," and the air division ended up sending down four people initially to work in the cell in the TACC and do electronic combat planning. And then one guy, they were going to rotate him out, and I was supposed to be going down for 45 day rotation, ended up staying 160.

When I first got there we just moved into a place called S-Con village. And what it was was a freight housing area that was never occupied. Outside of Riyadh, near the industrial sector and the guys that got there first, I mean when they first got there, you were talking no base and no office, nothing. They shoved them into hotels, I mean, sleeping in ballrooms, I mean it was just like, "Hey, got loads of people coming in, grab a Marriott Hotel and start filling them in wherever you can." They used empty storage rooms in basements and stuff like that. The guys that got there initially they had nothing to work with I mean, you know, what they brought in their bags and they were just basically building offices from scratch, places to work in, things like that.

I got there the end of September and the guys that were there before me had it pretty rough and everybody —the later you came the better off you had it. Initially like I said the guys were staying in hotels—20 people in the ballroom, sleeping on the floor, it was just a mess. I mean it wasn't like deploying to some place where you had this great, all these planes and pre-positioned stuff or something like that. It was show up and start working and do the best you can. People getting off the plane and going straight to work, stuff like that.

When we first got there the great thing was that everybody knew what had to be done. They were basically preparing for the defense of Saudi Arabia because the first priority was, "What if he decides to come across the border?" And that was, initially that was the number one priority, basically a defense, to come up with a defensive plan. How are you going to defend Saudi Arabia? With very little ground troops you're going to have to use a lot of air power. And most of the guys I was working with basically were worried about electronic combat aspect of that and, you know, how you going to keep their mobile SAMs from shooting down our airplanes while we're using the air support.

And airplanes were deploying in, basically we had some air defense assets there. Very few cass assets. You know they started coming in. As soon as somebody came in you had him to go frog, you know. We worked a lot with the Brits, extensively with the Brits. A lot with the Saudis. A lot with the Canadians later and a lot with the French.

The Brits and the Americans were attuned right off. The Brits came down from Germany. They're used to working with the Americans. The Saudis were pretty good, but with the Saudis it was more a . . . it wasn't a language barrier. Most of them spoke good English. It was kind a, you'd tell them what needed to be done kind of thing. With the Saudis it was pretty much leading them by the hand and saying, "Hey, you know, you need to put your AWACs here, you need to put this here, you know. And it was really a very good job of using everybody's assets. I mean like on AWACs there was nothing set up beforehand and they built the systems. A lot of the systems and things that would work in Europe didn't work down there. One of the things classical tactical air control center, things like that. You have your TACC and all your incorder stuff like that at Riyadh. The communications were terrible. Anything you wanted to do up by the border you couldn't talk to them on radio.

The coms over there, the coms were always a problem. You have a unit comes in and deploys into, you know, say, Dhahran or something like that or King Fahd or something like that. The first thing, how do you get the damn FRI to them. I mean, I'm serious. You didn't have an auditive line and all this other stuff set up I mean it took months just to get all the phones in place. And even after the war started the phones were a continuing problem.

The first SCUD attack we had I'll never forget because it was the second day of the war. The first night of the war we all worked. We knew what was going to happen. I went to work about midnight, sacked out on the floor for a couple of hours, got up about two o'clock in the morning just basically sat and waited for the response. Nothing really happened that night. The missions, everything went extremely well. It was a very, I will say the air campaign was extremely well planned and particularly the first three or four days because the idea was to take down the IADs first, the command and control, the key things you had to kill to get your airplanes in and out. It was very, very well orchestrated. The first raid was real classic. I mean with decoys and jamming assets and Wild

Weasels, command and control type targets, and a lot of things in the first three days like airplanes going in and wiping out a whole row of GCI sites so you didn't have to worry about them that.

The support from back home really made a difference, too. I mean Christmas time, packages, mail to Any Soldier. Really nice for a lot of guys it made things a lot easier. Especially before the war started you had guys there that had been there from August through December, just sitting there waiting for this deadline. They don't know if the war's going to start or not. They don't know if they're going to sit there for another six months. They don't know if Congress is going to pass something authorizing the use of force. It was really a, he couldn't bring the girls and stuff, just the idea that they got to bring a shirt over.

The big thing that was bothering the people the most before the war started was how long are we going to sit here while the politicians dick around. Can't say anything about Bush. He did exactly what needed to be done. He was, he told the military to come up with a plan, and use what they needed to use, and do it right and if they had run the show in Vietnam the way they ran it here, Vietnam would have turned out entirely different. They did it right this time. They did everything right from giving the military the go ahead to plan, to do everything they needed to do towards execution and letting the military do it. Then giving them the execution and the timing, the actual timing of it, the—I personally believe that we caught Saddam with his pants down.

I mean most of the guys, the security was very good, the average guy working in the headquarters did not know the attack was going to go when it did. The average guy on the front line did not know. On ours. And on his. The security was very good, and the timing of it, the Iraqis were not ready for it at all it was obvious. I mean, poor response. And the politicians played a big role in the surprise factor. I mean, the timing and the surprise and not a grudge will build up. Thing we did in Vietnam with "Okay today we can bomb bridges. You can't bomb SAM sites and you can bomb this, you can't bomb that." None of those kind of things.

We had coverage for rules of engagement. They really went out of their way. There were a lot of targets it would have been nice to hit and I can remember sitting and watching CNN and seeing Peter on CNN and saying, "Boy we sure would like put one in your basement buddy." And then it came out on the news later what was in his basement, but . . .

It seemed like after the air campaign and the psychological operations campaign, that the Iraqi army got. . . the regular army soldier welcomed the ground war because it gave him an opportunity to surrender because he's stuck out there in a hole getting bombed every night with everybody and he was just stuck between a rock and a hard place.

If you had an opportunity to surrender without the Republican Guard shooting in the back of your head and it's really a shame. We actually felt sorry for the Iraqi soldiers we were bombing because we knew they didn't want to be there and there wasn't much we could do about it. We were hitting the Republican Guard hard, as hard as we could. It was just a matter of we had to do it, but we actually felt sorry for them.

One of the things that was really unique about this was this was the first time they ever had all the precision bombing and the collateral damage was extremely limited because of the precise munitions used, especially in raids on Baghdad, things like that. The effect of this was that the average Iraqi didn't seem to understand that there was a war on. He was . . . in the first few days of the bombing campaign, you'd see people getting interviewed on CNN and their shops were open as normal. Everything was like optional in the city of Baghdad.

A block away there's a building destroyed but it didn't really affect the civilian populace. I don't think the civilian population of Baghdad initially understood that there was a war on and that we were bombing because we did such a precise job of doing it whereas years ago in World War II you'd go to a German city and you wanted to knock out a particular plant or something you'd send in a mass formation of B-26s and you bombed the whole area and you leveled a city and the population knew that there was a war on. I mean, it was really brought home to the civilian population. In this war it was entirely different, it was like the civilian population of Baghdad was isolated from the war and it was something the army had to deal with down in Kuwait or that because the bombing campaign never really impacted the civilian population until well into the campaign when the folks in Baghdad didn't have any gas, didn't have any water, didn't have any electricity. And then it started to affect their life, but initially the precision bombing was so good that it was almost like just an inconvenience to the average Joe in the street because he had to travel a block around where all the rubble was.

If we wanted to, we could have put, we could have taken the B-52s off the Republican Guard and put them over Baghdad and that would have got their attention. I guess that was not done.

On the personal side, there's a lot of folks that

deployed Desert Shield/Desert Storm from Germany. From Europe. They left behind a lot of dependents. And when everybody thinks about the military going to war and you think about all the rallies back home and all the family members back in the States, the family members who were left back in Germany really had it rough.

You're talking about a woman living on the German economy with or without kids, doesn't speak German, the whole unit goes. In our case, most of the people I work with went. And they're stuck out there by themselves, doing an overseas tour in the military is rough on the family anyhow. When you do any overseas tour the idea in Germany was "we're here to fight this NATO war" and if there's ever a war the guys'll stay and the dependents will all go back to the States. But here you have the guys going off to another country to do a war and the dependents are all stuck in Germany. They don't know when their husbands are coming back, they don't know when the war's going to start, they're under a lot of stress, a lot of pressure. They don't speak the language and they're stuck out there on the economy, and it's really rough on them.

ROGER ZAPATA

Rank: Lance Corporal
Service: Marine Corps
Duty: Infantry
Hometown: San Antonio, Texas

I think first of all, when we first landed there in early September, the heat was rather intense. I think it was punishing at times. The first couple of days we were at the hangar and got there and the heat was so intense that we laid in the cots and barely could move. We stripped down to PT shorts and PT shirts—the water itself would turn hot, you know—all that we had to clear our throats, I think just getting up to drink water was a serious task. It was definitely intense.

Being a marine, we only had roughly three days to go and then we got sent right to the field after that. And from there we dug in at night because the heat was too intense—the heat would rob your mind of thoughts. . . .

When we first got there our primary mission was to defend Saudi Arabia. Before we weren't sure if they were taking any kind of offensive. We knew it might be there somewhere in the background, but nothing had been passed down officially. So when we got there we set in, we dug in positions and the ground—where we dug in was pretty hard, so it took a while for us to dig in and we dug in, got ready, you know—everybody's mind was wondering you know, what's going to happen. And at night you know, there would be long processions of . . . people fleeing Kuwait because we were in the crotch—I don't know if you've heard that term—it's a six-lane highway where it would most likely be the area of approach. Pretty much everybody else was saying that if they were going to take Saudi Arabia, that would be the most likely avenue of approach, where they would come through . . . so at that place we set up our defensive positions and we dug in.

We dug in and we set up and we waited and you know, at night it would be long processions of vehicles fleeing Kuwait and from there it became more or less a waiting game, you know. We as being marines—you know, Hawaiian marines—we're a contingent force, we pretty much are . . . we have everything in Hawaii, so we're there, boom, ready to go. So we sat there and I guess a little bit of frustration started messing with the heat and all and we started hearing rumors about how, "The army's not ready, the army's not ready."

So we were like, "How does that affect us?" Because we're ready go. We want to get it over with. We figured we'd get it over with, we'd come home. The faster we'd get it over with, the faster we'd get home. And the waiting game began. You know, training and training. We'd do the mechanized training—constantly training, training, training. The same for almost every scenario possible, you know? We didn't really have any type of mount facilities—mount is what we call urban training. We didn't have that facility really around, so we built our own. We used racks, tents, tepee tents, anything our imagination could make into a building or an impact scene. We practiced taking it and clearing it. You know, from there, it was just more training. We'd take anything they'd throw at us.

We were ready to go, we were all trained. Uh, I guess everybody pretty much had it in their mind that if anything happened their best way of really stopping us would be gas, but we were prepared to fight dirty in the sense that if we got gassed, we were going to keep fighting until we had either secured our objective or pushed the enemies far enough back that we could stop and bring in decons because it wouldn't make any sense to stop our push forward. We wanted to keep the momentum going.

We saw POWs pretty much but we went in right behind Ripper, my company did—went in right behind Ripper and as soon as we came in there were POWs left and right. As we were going in most of the combat we saw was the Cobras and the RT's, you know, and they were just tearing things up. We also had the LEI's to our right. As soon as we went in they were pretty much . . . left and right. You know, we couldn't fire on them because they were surrendering. So we put them to the side and set up camps. At one time I had 70 POWs on the back of a truck...because there were so many of them. Some of them spoke pretty decent English though. A certain POW I recall, his name was Brian and he spoke almost perfect English. He told me he was from Chicago, that he was an American citizen and that he came home to visit his father and was forced to fight for Hussein.

I also had another POW that was in there and he was—I don't know, I couldn't really say if he was too pro—of course I had an automatic weapon in his face. I don't know if he was going to lie to me or not but he pretty much was saying he joined the military when he was fourteen years old, you know. He learned English in the military. He fought against Iran and more or less he was tired but when I mentioned that how would he feel if I told him Hussein was dead, he didn't really answer, he just kind of like, you know, looked away.

I told him—just to see what his reaction would be—I

told him that Basra and Baghdad were being bombed, that they were being pretty much wiped off the map. And some of the POWs broke out in tears. They were really in shock. That was my intent. We were trying to cool them out. The unit—I can't remember his name—they told me the unit, that most of the POWs on the back of that truck were all in the same unit. They had been together since they were fourteen years old. And these men had fought against Iran for eight years.

I think also I heard somewhere along the line on the radio, that they weren't equipped properly. That's a big negative. When we went through there, through some of their bunkers, they had some serious weapons. Some of their weapons were immaculate. I mean just clean—ready to go, they just needed a fight—but you know, they just didn't fight. They didn't want to fight, they didn't have the will to fight. I don't think they could have contended against us.

I definitely think the bombing had a lot to do with that. We were ready in a sense but I guess it also did well for the troop morale because I went in there with a good feeling knowing that they got their fair share of the bombing, you know. I had it in my mind that they did get bombed well and that if there was anything left, well then they weren't going to stand very much against us. There was also a saying in our platoon that you know, you could bomb the hell out of a city, you could shell the hell out of hill, but neither are yours until grunt puts a flag on it. So we all believed that too, you know? But, not to take anything away from the flyboys—they did a hell of a job, you know.

The thing that sticks, though, is maybe the cause. You know? And also maybe the fact that I have little nephews and nieces and my platoon commander put my name in a city paper—my hometown city paper—and I had little kids writing me and my thought for that was if this enemy is not destroyed now, ten years from now he'll have nuclear capability and instead of the enemy being destroyed now while we had the means and we had the ability to destroy him now, he'll be fighting my little nephews and these little children that are in classes right now who are wondering what's going on and writing this letter to support—not even understanding the pain and the hate that we went through—would have to be doing what I can accomplish now.

But yet they'd face a worse and greater enemy because he would have nuclear capability. So that stayed in the back of my mind. I really thought—you know, I really believed in the cause. There was no doubt in my mind that the enemy had to be destroyed so that I didn't have any problems when they said "Let's go, it's time to do it."

CHARLES E. HALSTEAD

Rank: Specialist
Service: Army
Duty: Infantry
Hometown: Ogden, Kansas

My unit, my mother unit was Delta 516. Infantry. I was cross-attached to—well, my whole company was—to the 234 Armor, which made up the 234 Armor Task Force. Tanks. Tanks and Bradley. And of course your artillery. I'm with a Bradley. The Bradley is mechanized infantry, which means for the infantry to get up to the main portion of the battle in a hurry without wearing out the infantry. It has 25-millimeter main guns, which is used both for armor and personnel. Also a 7.62 machine gun. And a TOW missile.

It will definitely do a number on a tank. As far as what we did there, we basically led the task force. My company. We fought three major battles when I was there. We did the breach in Southern Iraq. Okay, that was my task force. Just before we got to the breach, we had an objective, which was the trench line, which my platoon was to clear. We didn't meet any resistance there. They surrendered pretty much immediately. We just had—we fired a couple of rounds over the top of their heads, and we had to fire a couple into some bunkers to force them out.

We spent about a half a day there, processing the POWs, because there were 187. They were in bad shape. They hadn't eaten or had water in about four days. Some of them, we made them come to us for our safety. Some of them crawled, had to crawl. Couldn't even walk. Some of them, just as they got to us, collapsed. At which time we started hooking IVs into them, getting them medical treatment the best we could, and getting them out to the hospitals. Some were in better shape, and we tied their hands and put them on stretchers and sent them also to the rear.

The last battle was with the Republican Guard. That was our hardest battle. We rode around—well, we fought them in approximately 19 hours. That was the last battle. Through the four days of the war, we travelled 140 miles, in the Bradleys. When we did the breach, that was the only time we wore gas masks, when we did the breach. We took a little bit of resistance there. Not much, small arms fire. Then we caught the Republican Guard. We took small arms fire from them, but they couldn't see us. That's the only reason we took small arms fire.

They couldn't see us through the night sights of the Bradleys. And also the EPWs said that they didn't know what the Bradley was. So they didn't fire anything heavy. Like I say, they could only see us about 500 meters out, where we could see them a long ways. And that was pretty much the extent of that. It was like driving down a range. Pretty much.

The thing that will stand out most, that I'll remember most, was watching a man get blowed up, from the main gunner on our Bradley. We were in contact, and I'm not sure whether he was trying to surrender or what it was, but he come up out of the hole, and one of the gunners popped him with a 25-millimeter.

Everyone in my company survived. We had a couple of guys minorly injured. One was from a fire extinguishing unit in the Bradley that went off, and he tried to get out of the way of it, because when it goes off, it will burn, it will burn you. And he busted his head open. And another one had an ammo box bounce out and break his foot.

The only burnings that I've seen are the oil wells. About half of them were black smoke. The other half were white smoke. Now, of a day, if the wind shifted and blew smoke towards us, it was almost—it would get dark from the smoke so we'd have to turn on the lights on the vehicles.

The first time—we moved out from the MGM, that's where I stayed when we first got into Saudi. We moved out from there on the 12th of January. That's what we called the dorms where they had us at. And we moved out into the desert. The first night we were there, it rained. We were all cold and wet. That was the 12th of January. I mean, we got soaked, everybody. Everything we had was wet and everything.

Then we got orders to move out on a combat mission. We thought that the Republican Guard was coming at us. And we left all of our gear. I mean, people left sleeping bags, everything, it was just a spur of the moment thing. And we found out the next morning that it was just a false alarm. After that, we moved up into a training—or a PAA, and we set up there, and like I say, we had left gear, so that made things miserable for us. When it rained we were cold, we were wet. The chow wasn't that good sometimes. And neither was the mail. So morale kind of went—it fluctuated up and down, you know. Before the war started, just before the war.

I went to sleep the night before the bombing was started. And I was in the bag asleep when the lieutenant ran in, because we took our tarps and made roofs to keep the rain off of us. And he ran in and told us that we were Redcom 1, weapons were free. And everybody immediately, I mean, no questions asked, up out of the bags, we're in the Bradley, loaded up—at the time we weren't even loaded up with our weapons, they just weren't loaded. We loaded up our weapons systems, and prepared our night sights. Night vision goggles. And I was raised up over the back of the Bradley and I was sort of looking up, and I could see the flashes, you know, the bombings that was going on, and the anti-aircraft tracers going up into the air. I was scared. We had no idea what was going on. We knew before that they had—we thought they had planned to attack us, and this is what we were thinking was going on, until our battalion commander came over the radio and told us exactly what was happening.

This—it was about two hours after it had started that we got the word that they were bombing Baghdad and everything. Everybody was pretty much scared. But they were ready. We were ready. I knew I could do the job because we had two missiles—like I say, our weapons weren't loaded and I had two missiles laying on the outside of my Bradley on the back, and my gunner said that was the quickest he'd ever seen two missiles get loaded in his life. Because I had them loaded in, like, 15 seconds.

In my company I think there were probably 110 or 115 men. We were between about 50 and 75 meters apart. I'm the loader on the Bradley and I have a CVC back in the back with me. A CVC is a set of headphones basically with a mike. It's a helmet, it's got the headphones and mike. I had it on and the gunner, of course, had his on, and the driver. And we were all communicating, talking, you know. When I couldn't see what was going on, I was asking them if maybe they could and everything. But then I was smoking one cigarette right after the other, too. We were comforting each other.

And then I ran out of cigarettes after about a month out

there. I ran out and I was out for about a week and my friends who had extra cigarettes would give them to me. And then the PX truck came by and we bought them off the PX truck.

They had Finance that would come around to each unit and we could draw our casual pay from Finance. But the way I did it was that I had my wife send it to me.

I have three children. When I left, they took it pretty hard. And that's one of the reasons I'm going back now on emergency leave. It was really rough on my kids. One's nine, my oldest daughter. I've got a son that's five and a daughter that's 13 months. My wife was in a support group, along with a couple of lieutenants' wives and a couple of sergeants in my company. They broke it down, I think, throughout my company. Like, each town, say Junction City, Kansas—the wives that lived in that area formed a group. The wives that lived in the Manhattan, Kansas area formed a group. And they continued to call each other and let each other know what was going on, which was a big help to them.

TODD R. STANDARD

Rank: Captain
Service: Marine Corps
Duty: F/A 18 Hornet Pilot
Hometown: Pennsis, Missouri

The first mission that we had was kind of scary. We used a computer, which determines how dangerous your mission is and not knowing how bad it was and stuff like that, it had—the machine indicated we had a slim chance of surviving the mission that we were going on. We had to take out a command and control site inside of Iraq and we flew part of about a 20-30 plane strike group, just Hornets with HARM shooters and two 786Bs for escorts and we took out—the place that we destroyed is like, it had AWSs around it.

It just depends upon the pilot, but the Hornet just bombs them right where you want them. I was scared. I did manage to get some sleep but it was kind of difficult on the way up there. I'd never been so scared to the point where I almost felt like I was getting sick. We were still in good guy country but we were about to cross the lines. My stomach was hurting and I thought, I can't believe I'm doing this. You know, you go through your whole career training and stuff like that and all of a sudden it's actually happening. And you didn't know how bad the war was going to be. And it was the first daylight strike into Iraq.

Actually it was the first day, because a couple of the guys had the night strikes. But I think daytime is more scary because you don't feel like you're protected as much. The guys in my squadron and they said the triple A was unbelievable. There was only one person in my squadron who had been in Vietnam, and that was the skipper. We didn't have a guy in the squadron who had under 400 hours in the aircraft. I mean we didn't have any real young guys who weren't good in the plane. The squadron average was probably about seven or 800.

What we'd normally do was we'd go into a target area. We did all the tasks where I'd take on the command control first off and then moved in to support the marines and the deltas got to come in and use our binoculars in the back, keep moving it around, find the target and mark it with a little beep force, and we kind of served a little wagon on top of them and with singles or double, like marking trees into it or Rockeyes into targets and we did some real good work. I mean—around Basra it was unbelievable.

I think we just—as a lot of people said—we took away their EW assets. They didn't know—I think somebody's out there, but we had jammers up all the time. They didn't know when or who or how many and in what direction, I mean we had so many HARMs in the air too, it was unbelievable. Then we came in and there were multiple HARMs, high-speed anti-radiation missiles, covering the tarp. A good piece of gear.

Just to hit something with, we liked Mark 83s. The 83s are a thousand-pounder. That's what we prefer to carry. We normally deal with a double bubble with two drop tanks most of the time. And just like the Navy did, we can carry five 83s like that, so it's 5,000 pounds. We were up by about 12—ten or 12.

We saw probably a row of some of them underneath us and we had the altitude. We stayed well above the triple A and it was hard to see during the day. The guys who—there were some people who didn't know any better then to do the triple A and got nailed. It was worse than that in most of the places—around Basra and stuff it was heavier. Somebody had later engaged us this was going on around Basra and it was kind of cloudy you know, on the way up there, but we came in. They called us the icicles from hell, because your infrared signal is coming straight down at 30,000 feet, you pull back idle so it comes straight down, and pull it back so they can get a tone on you up and down.

From 30,000 feet, it's part of . . . would light the burners and rolling on a pure vertical straight down. You could look at the target and adjust it a little bit. You know, adjust your destination a couple of times and then pull your nose up a little bit and go up to 45, so you have a little air to ground range, as you go up to 20,000 feet and dream about how gutsy you are or until you acquire the target, do one last estimation and then lift them off. We would pull six or seven g's coming off target.

We dropped 84s that day. Two thousand pounders. I could see what I hit but it was too . . . It made a heck of a bang when it hit but you couldn't really tell because they were real small. You would pull up and you could see the explosion. I wasn't really caring about what blew up, I was looking for missiles and other planes, because there were planes everywhere. I saw a couple of SAMs go underneath but other than that, it's hard to see triple A during the day. But at night time you can see it pretty good.

I got some contacts, ran down a couple of Iranian helos. They got close to the ship, so we ran down the Iranians and they weren't talking to anybody. During night time it was VID, visual I.D. sighting, and head of

VID needs somebody at night—somebody—it's kind of hard to tell—what somebody is at night.

We were lucky. We got there late. We got there about December 16th and most of the unit is still there right now. We flew the Hornets in. It was hard on the families. My wife's a little bit better off. She's in the Navy, so she kind of has a better understanding of what's going on. She was just scared you know, she had her family around, always calling her and stuff like that.

We had no problems with keeping the canopies over them to keep from scratching and stuff like that, and a little bit of dust inside, but they just changed the lubricant that they used. The Hornet just proved how tough it was. This is why it was designed alone against some of the hand-helds and stuff like that. I had friends who had their blowers, their cans blown off both of them. Flew back single-engined 200 miles and landed the aircraft.

The Hornet has its after-burner cans stick real far out — the nozzles—and that's the primary heat source and most of the Russian missiles, the newer hand-helds will hit the heat source, hit them and just blow them off so it doesn't destroy the aircraft. Two of them came back with both their cans blown off with one engine shut down and you know, 190 knots, landed and the guy came back with a big hole blown in the bottom of one of his engines, did some triple A on the left wing tank and shattered it and set off ordnance on the rails, hooked up on the rail. He didn't jettison or anything. He didn't know what it was. He thought he was on fire . . .

They had all the escape and evasion plans. Like when to talk and as things come out, you know, what to do when they're trying to catch you. We had briefs from the air force SAR guys and the . . . real high-tech helicopter they had . . . what they use in the book—Tom Clancy's novel.

A lot of people—when the reports of coalition POWs started, were talking along the lines of "save your seat when you go," you know, keep dry, don't even worry about it; because there were all the horror stories of the things they were going to do to you and what they did to the Iranians and stuff. But I think cooler heads kind of prevailed after the first day. I don't think anyone really did that. But there was a lot of talk about that for a while. The scariest thing was that you didn't know what they were going to do to you.

Now the tanks were to be set down in some type of revetments, something semi-circular . . . and it'd just be sitting there and most of the time during the day they wouldn't run out, they'd have Rockeye or Mark 83s and a close Rockeye would take them out and hit the gas drums on the back and just blow the tops of them off. It was quite impressive to see them.

We got called in a couple of times for counter-battery suppression. Some unit will be getting incoming fire from an Iraqi unit. They have the capability of saying "here comes a shell, look at it through the radars and other assets and see where it's coming from." They'd pinpoint best they can and see that "hey, these guys are shooting at us," we'd type the numbers in where it is, the grid and stuff, then we'd run in and we'd hit it.

We pretty much just worked with other marines, but as for just Hornet pilots in general, it was really kind of amazing that you could fly with guys from squadrons on the east coast, west coast—because we're a Hawaii squadron—and we do exactly the same thing, we're all on the same sheet of music and it was really nice.

I think I understood the rules of engagement but I think some things in regard to the command structure had to be redone. They had to put a little more money into some of their things like their datalink and stuff like that. Did you hear about the road north of the highway of death? That was our squadrons that hit it—it was something like 30 miles of wreckage. I put five 83s right down the center of the road and got some secondaries and my third sortie, I don't know what the heck it hit but it whited out the target.

It's pitch black out. We go in with our lights off and it's kind of hard. The day we launched—we launched all the airplanes as soon as the sun started to come up but it was old run around, kind of . . . by altitude and we just had our lights on. You see someone, this little flash, or use our radar air-to-air to tell where we are. It was kinda scary. Big sky little bullet theory. You could see it on the board, pretty much. It was amazing to be in mid-air during the war. We went pretty much fifty-some days without a day off.

It worked real nice but there's a lot of things on the Hornet that need to be improved. If it was a more capable enemy that we fought against, they'd need to put some more money into the aircraft. There were a few problems that they had. They changed our software, for one thing, right before the war started, I mean, it's like '50s-'60s technology. . . .

GORDON SINCLAIR

Rank: Civilian
Hometown: St. Paul, Minnesota

My son is a first lieutenant in a, in one of the Marine regiments in the first division and of course when this whole crisis broke open, we were scared to death. Because we had read so much about the powerful Iraq army with their 500,000 men and 5,000 tanks, and endless artillery and all dug in inside of Kuwait. We thought that Bush was biting off an awful big chunk to tackle something like that.

And then, on the other hand, I kind of thought that, well, all the services have been training and they've been preparing for this and getting paid for it, so they've got to be sitting some place so maybe they might just as well go over there as to be sitting around the States forever and get some use out of all the money we spent and all the preparation that the troops have had. And that maybe depending on our special forces and our special weapons that maybe we can get in there and clean them out in a hurry. And the way it's turned out, of course, is just exactly that.

So now we're very, very happy to see that our servicemen have performed so wonderfully and we're all very proud of them, of course. We were planning to go back to the Twin Cities, but we're going to stay out here now and hope that they'll get back here soon enough so that we can welcome him here. I know he'll be very surprised to see us and it's going to be a very great and wonderful day when that happens.

I have two other children, but this is our son who is—he went through college and didn't have any immediate prospects so he decided to—he was always interested in the Marine Corps because I was in the Marine Corps, too, during World War II so as long as he could get a commission he went ahead and joined the Marines and he's loved it. He's liked every minute of it. But he's been on the go so much transferring around that it's actually kind of hard to keep track of where he is at any time.

He's kind of closemouthed. He doesn't have a whole lot to say, you know, anything that was, he didn't say anything more than what was, than what we read in the newspaper. But I guess it was fairly good living conditions considering that it wasn't 130 degrees and you know it was raining and it was cool and it was wet. And I think that was a whole lot better than trying to do that battle in midsummer when it was so beastly hot so it looks to me like we got in there and are getting out at just the very right time.

When the war started, of course, I thought the same as everybody else thought: just holding our breath, hoping that it wasn't going to be a disaster, hoping that it wouldn't be another Vietnam and drag on for months and months, years and years. And hoping that Hussein was a big bag of air with the way he was pushing his propaganda at us. And happily that's the way it did turn out.

You know, when I was in the Marine Corps in World War II, all of our assaults were head on, there was no room on those islands to maneuver and so it was just push, push, push straight ahead all the time. We suffered terrible casualties compared to what this operation has done. And of course we didn't have those sophisticated weaponry. We had a lot of air cover but the air cover wasn't pinpoint accurate the way it is today. And there was no room for maneuver, you just had to go in there with the flame throwers and the satchel charges and blast those guys out of their caves. And it was mountainous, too, in many places, you know, and really tough fighting. Now here in the Gulf the, of course, the two Marine divisions they did go straight ahead, but the maneuvering by the Army was marvelous the way they circled around behind and when they got there I guess they found that most of the troops were dead. They didn't have all that opposition anyway. But the marines did have some tough opposition at the air field and at Kuwait City.

Of course, we wouldn't know whether they should bomb longer or not but the military I'm sure had a good feeling that that was enough, that now was the time to go so I have all the confidence in the world in those commanding generals over there. They did a marvelous job.

STEVE A. BROWN

Rank: Sergeant
Service: Army
Duty: Airborne
Hometown: Kent, Ohio

Well, at first it was like—at first it was very boring. You know, the long wait was very boring and very hard on all the troops and stuff. We trained more there than we do back, you know, back in the garrison. We covered almost every type of training there is as far as, you know, the different categories of training there, where I think we are proficient in everything right now.

Our initial movements, you know, we went in the day before Ground Day. And I searched personally about 45, and that type of war is too personal for me, because you knew—I mean, there were thousands just coming with their hands up and stuff. And you knew from their faces and stuff, and they were crying, and some of them mad and some of them proud, but some of them were scared for their life. It was just too personal for me, because you start getting like choked up and stuff.

All of us felt sorry, felt compassion, felt sad that they had to go through with what they did because of some idiot like Hussein that was pushing them. Because obviously they didn't want to fight. I would say searching those prisoners will stay with me the rest of my life, because some of them, you know, you have one guy searching them and the other guy has them at gunpoint, and some of them just totally thought they were going to die, you know, because they had us built up so bad. And there was one instance where one of the prisoners asked an officer, how many people he had to kill to get his Airborne tabs. So, you know, the propaganda and that kind of stuff, I've learned, I mean, I've been waking up to it, it's kind of—you know, it goes both ways. We did ours, but it got them. We do it pretty good. They do it to get their troops, their heads going the other way. So I'm sure they really think the 82nd is something.

JEFFREY W. HOLCOMB

Rank: Private First Class
Service: Marine Corps
Duty: Infantry
Hometown: Poulsbo, Washington

We arrived in Saudi Arabia January 19, 1991. At first, there was a lot of boredom, broken up by the few days that the war actually took place. We were at the airport at, I forgot which airbase it was, I believe it was Norton. And we were watching TV when the air raids started.

It was like, "Oh, my God, it's finally happening! We're going to be there!" It was a rush, yet it was scary. You weren't sure what was going to happen. We stepped off the airplane and you looked down and you see the sand for miles even at night and you knew that anytime a missile could come in and you weren't sure quite where you were going to be camping out or how close to the enemy you were going to be and . . .

It was deep anxieties, I mean "fear" is not quite the word for it. Because you didn't really know what to be scared of, but getting up at guard duty in the middle of the night with the locked and loaded weapon, knowing that anytime something could happen . . . you knew that this was it, this is what you'd been training for.

In the middle of the night you normally had a two-man sentry team that roamed the camp area to make sure that nobody came in and bothered the camp. Our first camp was probably about 300 yards long, maybe 30 meters wide or so.

Every day, you'd always see planes flying in and out

from bombing raids and you knew where they were going. And every once in a while you could see a flash or you could hear a boom and feel the ground move and you, you knew it was for real. Kind of like a small tremor for an earthquake for Caifornia. It was just weird. It was like you knew that there was a bomb, you know, your own forces creating this, this disturbance in the earth. It was maybe a second or two. Just brief. But it just, it was long enough to let you know that it was there.

My platoon went up and helped liberate Al-Jabar airport which was south of Kuwait City. It was, at that point it was scary. Because you knew that there was enemy in this airport and we had surrounded most of the airport and we were just waiting to go in. And then as the actual invasion took place, my platoon, we did a scouting mission around the outside to make sure no POWs were escaping. And it was just, you could hear the gunfire and the artillery going off and hitting the airport. You could watch the explosions. It was, it was different. I don't know. It's unexplainable. You knew that you could die any minute. You didn't know what was going on.

My family was scared the whole time I was over there, even after the war was over because my father served in Vietnam and he knew that at any time something could erupt again. My dad was in the Navy.

The airport that we overtook was destroyed. It was. I mean, the Iraqis had, you know, they had taken everything they could out of it and then our artillery had devastated it. There was holes everywhere from artillery and munitions and buildings were destroyed, just toppled. It was mines everywhere. It was incredible. It was awe-inspiring.

Our platoon had gone up and done a breaching of the minefields and we were going up and look for the best route through and then they brought in the demolitions people to blow the mines up and we'd mark the routes with chemical lights. I believe they were French-made anti-tank mines. The were approximately, I'd say, almost a foot across.

They were enough to destroy a tank. They shot line charges across the mine fields. The rockets going across with the little, I believe it was C-4 charges hooked to it. And they all blew up at once and blew the minefield across enough for a road to get through.

We'd go through. We'd mark the road, the borders so people knew where to drive and walk. Then the soot came in. The first time we noticed it was when right before we started breaching the minefields. And it came in. It was like a thick fog only it was black and it, when we first experienced it, I believe it was going on four in the afternoon and it was blacker than even your eyes closed. It was so black you couldn't see your hand. It was incredible. It was devastating. It rolled in like a fog bank. It was just, it was amazing. It came in from in front of us. It just engulfed us.

At times it fluctuated. At different times it came in and out. It was just, it was scary because you couldn't even see a inch in front of your face. You had no idea where you were. Even with the night vision devices it was impossible to see.

We just stopped at that point. When you couldn't see you didn't move. Because it was too dangerous. We knew there was too many hazards around us to try to move. My platoon did go in and secure some bunkers on the north side of Al-Jabar airport.

The bunkers are basically just eight to ten foot holes in the ground with, some of them had aluminum or plywood coverings on them covered with sand. We'd normally send in two people, one with a 9mm and one with an M-16 to cover the holes. The man with the 9mm would move in to cover the tunnel and make sure there was nobody inside. And then we'd move in and make sure there was no booby traps in the entrance. Little by little we'd pull piece by piece out with string or 550 cord so that we wouldn't set off any booby traps. My team didn't but one team in my platoon did set off a booby trap. Nobody got hurt, though.

If I had to say the one thing that will stick with me, it would be one word: sand. That's, it just, endless, endless sand. It was incredible. Devastation, that's another word. Like when we moved in, we did go through Kuwait City. And the devastation on the outskirts and the blown up tanks and vehicles were just incredible.

When we crossed the berm separating Saudi Arabia and Kuwait that first day the ground war started, it was, it actually hit that it was real. Because up to that point we had done nothing beyond the berm. We'd been to the berm and we'd watched and you know set up observation points but it still was more like a training mission than an actual live thing and then the day we crossed the berm it really hit you. It was like, this is real, you know, you could die. It was, like I said, it was anxiety more than fear. It was different.

Everyone stuck together and did what they were supposed to do. A few let down more than I thought they would, they weren't quite as rambunctious in the face of things, but as far as my unit, I mean, being in recon, it's all a volunteer basis to be here, so it's not like being in a regular grunt unit where you're just thrown in there and have to do it.

So everybody here, I mean, wanted to be here so it's not, there's really no letting down in the face of things.

Then we started getting the EPWs. Almost right away.

You go through their personal gear making sure there's nothing they can have that would lead to their revolt or anything. Religious items and such you, we normally put them in like a ziploc baggie and showed them that we were going to hold them for them and not hurt them. And then normally they would come along quietly. So specifically they had this one article, I'm not sure what it was called, it was a little block. It kind of looked like a bar of soap. And they used it to pray with. And when you took this out of their knapsack or whatever they had, they'd really go crazy if you'd throw it around because you know I guess it was their most important holy item. Kind of like a cross would be to one of our soldiers, or a bible. A little block like tannish color or white. Kinda looked like a bar of soap, but to them it was a really, they use it, they put their foreheads on it when they bow. I'd only seen one block and it was white, it looked like a bar of Ivory soap.

At that point we were dug in inside of Al-Jabar airport. After the war got over and we heard it was done and at that point we were just sitting around waiting to go to leave to go back into Saudi Arabia. There wasn't much as far as our platoon went, there wasn't anything to do except for clear the bunkers and that's when we went out and started clearing bunkers. Making sure there was no POWs left.

We left within four days of the war being over. We had secured the airport within hours and then left, I think it was four days after the war ended.

When it ended, it was incredible. It almost made you want to cry at points. I mean, the people in Kuwait were so exhuberant about us being there and saving their country. It was incredible. They were handing us turbans and flags and articles of clothing and we were handing them back American flags and it was touching.

NANCY E. BRENNAN

Rank: Lieutenant Commander
Service: Navy
Duty: Nurse
Hometown: Henderson, North Carolina

I was actually doing two days a month with the Navy Reserves and then working part time at the Coronado Emergency Room in Coronado. Going from part time or per diem nursing to full time was quite different. The number of hours with working 12 hour shifts versus four and a half to six hour shifts part time and per diem. So it was sort of full time and 12 hours shifts and it was quite a difference within family life.

I have one child that's eight, a little boy, and thankfully he's in school from 8:00 to 2:15 so that helped matters quite a bit. I was on active duty for three years and I've been in the reserves for something like ten years. I never thought this would happen.

Actually, it had some positive aspects with having an eight year old and me working per diem that I was able to go back and work full time and see how it would react with my whole family life and knowing that my husband pitched in and helped out that I know that I can go out there and since he's still only eight feel comfortable with working full time.

I'll definitely stay in the reserves. A part of me is very patriotic and part of me is very military oriented and I enjoy the reserves and I think I'll always stay in until I'm in there for 20. I know a lot of people have had hardships and you know have thought once this is all over I'll get out and I'll stay out, but I think because the transition went so smoothly with the reserves just filling in to the active duty billets and everybody being pretty well satisfied that I think more people will stay in than had originally thought to get out.

I know that there were people that had drilled and mobilized, their mobilization station was Balboa, and they were sent to Long Beach and there were people from Long Beach that were sent down to Balboa. There were people in Oakland—the whole hospital in Oakland was completely taken out and put on the Mercy. There were reserve Oakland nurses that actually were there at Oakland and they didn't call a single one of them. And they called San Diego Naval Hospital nurses and they were sent to Oakland to completely reactivate and open the hospital whereas they should have taken Oakland reserve nurses and put them there and kept the San Diego nurses at home. It was a possibility that I could have gone to Saudi Arabia. The Mercy, Oakland, Bethesda, Portsmouth—anywhere.

My husband is a financial advisor, but he was a marine for a couple of years in the '60s so he actually understands military life, but he travels quite a bit with his work so that was, that was one of the biggest problems we had to work through was he being out of town, I working 12 hours shifts and am I going to get a sitter for two hours in the morning from six to eight o'clock. I mean, who wants to come from six to eight o'clock in the morning? And if he's gone at night, somebody's going to have to come over and spend the night at my house. So the hours really created a problem, although lately he hadn't traveled quite as much and this transition has been quite smooth.

I was actually called Valentine's Day, February 14, and

I was actually signed to get my green card February 22. I've been active duty since. I'll probably be there until about the middle of May.

All the reserve nurses were called together to have a meeting with Admiral Stratton and overall I'd say three-quarters of the nurses seemed to be satisfied where they were. There were a lot of nurses that were put in areas where they had never worked. They were emergency room nurses and they were sent to the critical care units. They were jail nurses that worked outside in the jail and they were sent to critical care areas where they basically had never done that before. They were public health nurses that worked out in the public health field that were sent to the emergency room or the critical care areas whereas they don't have the experience for that. There were nurses that were put on permanent nights with families and stuff like that that basically, you know, there were hardships with that, but I think overall people were sent to the areas that they best were suited for, they had 701 people come into the hospital, they had 500 to leave and with the influx of people they were not able to quickly find out where everybody normally worked or what their area was. I mean, basically at that point they were just trying to fill spaces. They knew these casualties were coming in, we need so many people in the medicine floor, hey, we've got this body, this body, this body. The people they knew they tried to put in the areas they could otherwise they just basically put bodies in areas.

Basically in those particular areas they did do some on-the-job training. Although there were memos that went out that said, "We would like in a happening like this again how many of you are actively working in the hospitals on the side? Do you all work in clinics? How often do you work? Do you work full time, part time, per diem? How long have you been out of the nursing field?" So they had two nurses that were in education and training that basically were set aside to basically think about starting up a complete workshop for all these nurses that really needed excess training in order to just basically start working.

But they did have some on-the-job training. If you had not worked in certain areas then they basically quickly trained you. I know they had meetings with all the hospitals in the outside to know their capabilities of handling trauma patients. What are your bed capabilities? How many beds do you have on outside in case we do get an influx of people we're going to start sending them out. They were just going to basically say start clearing out Balboa, the naval hospital in San Diego, and clearing it out and bring out all the casualties there.

One thing I learned from all this, and that's that the reserves can do it if they need to do it. And I think they proved to the Navy and the whole military and the Air Force, Marines or whatever, Army, that so many people have basically come to the reserves and said that, you know, as you come in to do your two weeks or your two days a month or whatever, you know, you're sort of labeled as a reserve although we have come in now and seen the reserve people step in and you would not know that they are reserves. You would think that they were active duty on board and you would never know the difference.

But there are always problems that come up in something this big. There was a nurse that went to Oakland that basically went up there and said she was to start on a ward. A ward is basically a nursing unit that has so many beds to take care of, say, medical people, surgery people, general surgery, urology, whatever. There may be 30 to 40 beds on a unit and she was to go up there and basically start from scratch to work on this unit. Apparently, the nurses that were in the hospital had taken all the manuals, policies, procedures, everything from the ward. They had basically nothing. They had to make the beds, find the linen. Start making policies and procedures and find the lab chits and here they had this influx of people continually to open up the ward for people being admitted to the hospital and had to start from scratch to do everything because everything had been taken off the ward. Basically, it boils down to going to a lot of empty rooms with just a bed there and having to start and go from there.

BRENT C. DRAGILA

Rank: Private First Class
Service: Army
Duty: Light Armor
Hometown: Auburn, California

Basically, our mission was to provide security for the main task force while they moved up and also before the ground war of just basically keeping, just basic, you make sure they weren't going to attack. I arrived on January 16th.

The night we were supposed to fly out we got cancelled because bombing started that night. It started making me think a lot about what things that I wish I had done before I was getting ready to go and made me have a little more better outlook on life, probably just because I wish I could go back and redo a few things. Just possibly doing more things with family members and sometimes I felt that I kind of shunned them off and did things, kind of just didn't pay much attention to them. I thought I should have maybe put a little more emphasis on spending time with them.

Everyone was hyped up, seemed to be hyped up, and I mean, there was a lot of doubt going through our mind of what it was going to be like, but everyone was functioning fine and everyone had real good morale and seemed to be really up on everything and just basically wanted to make sure that we were careful and didn't make any major mistakes on our own part. We figured we'd be all right.

I went into the Kuwaiti International Airport after the

Iraqis had been there for six months. There wasn't much there by the time I got to the actual airport. But the Iraqis were real sloppy as far as where they went to the bathroom. They went to the bathroom just everywhere, they really didn't have like a designated place. They were just, they weren't very sanitary. And it was real, things were pretty well torn up.

It made me, it made you realize that those people had their own little world just like these people back here in the States have. And, I mean, it'd be strange to see blown up tanks in downtown L.A. or I mean any town like they did and just it pretty much put their world upside down. It kinda made you realize that.

We moved when we first, before the ground war, actually, about a month and a half before the ground war, we were on the berm and there was a mechanized unit of tanks coming at us. Iraqi tanks. And so I was down in my hole sleeping and everyone started yelling and you know it kind of hit me just the fact it kinda felt a little bit hopeless and weird, trying to go the other way.

We were pretty much isolated on the berm, basically by ourselves and that day LAI units moved up and were getting ready to take over our postion and that's the night that everything went off and we, we just basically, we went the other way. And we saw the LAI get hit, that's a light armored vehicle, one of those rubber tired, carries like five or six guys with it, it's basically like a personnel carrier. They use it a lot for recon out there 'cause they were pretty effective in the desert, I guess.

Well, we drove right past it. Apparently, it was one that got hit by one of our own planes. An A-10 hit it and we drove right past it. It was on fire and there's another vehicle on the right, I'm not sure what it was, but we drove right past it and just looking at it and realizing there was people that'd just died right there a couple minutes before we were there. Kinda made me realize that things were definitely for real.

When we first went in to the oil where the actual smoke was, when you drove into the smoke it was night. It was just like you were in nighttime, you had to have your headlights on or stay real close to the vehicle and finally it was just being in nighttime. It was like night again and as far as the smoke, the smoke didn't hurt your lungs or anything. We did get, drive by a couple of oil wells that blew up, they were on fire so they were just shooting oil out and it just covered our vehicles with black, just the windows and everything, just solid black, just oil just dripping off.

Showering was a problem. We tried to bathe with little small amounts of water whenever we had the chance or time, but most of the time as far as actually taking showers, we take a shower maybe once a month. And it was pretty hard to get a shower because we really didn't have a designated camp where they had showers set up so we had to borrow showers and sometimes it was hard to get put in the schedule. There are different types. Some are like a big GP tent, it's a big green tent that you walk in and it had a bunch of, you know, an area to undress in, then it's a bunch of stalls, and then there's other kinds where you pour the water in the top and then it's like a port-a-potty and it had an actual faucet on it, but you put water in the top before you take a shower.

What I remember, just the fact that, it seemed to me that to the Iraqis life wasn't very valuable. Life was, it was no big deal for someone to die to them and it made me realize that, appreciate what I have here and just be able to do everyday things a lot more that a lot of people just take for granted—just being able to drive down to the local pizza parlor and buy a pizza and drink a beer and watch TV or something that you didn't get over there and it kinda made you realize how nice it is to be able to do that.

WILLIAM F. STRUEVER

Rank: Staff Sergeant
Service: Marine Corps
Duty: Supply
Hometown: Cincinnati, Ohio

I joined the Marine Corps June of 1975 and I'm currently attached to the 3rd Battalion 9th Marines. I'm the Supply Chief. I went into Kuwait City with our battalion and I started off with our battalion too. We originally went to Jubayl, Port of Jubayl, August 19. We were involved, I was in supply, involved in offloading the MPS ships.

It was real hot. Humidity at Jubayl Port was real bad. The command was coordinating where we were to go and then when we finally went into the desert it was a lot cooler because the humidity went down. It seemed like it was cooler because it was less humidity. It was better for us and better for the troops and everything.

They have a list of what an infantry battalion rates and we would basically go there and draw what we needed, what we didn't bring over we'd draw supplies to bring us up to what we needed to fulfill our combat needs. We stayed out in the field with our battalions. It was initially only 20 miles from Jubayl, I guess. We were in one of the first breaching battalions.

We started off. We went in. Okay, I was with Task Force Papa Bear, that was tanks. We had two rifle companies with us and we, I was back probably two miles. I didn't initially. When we first started off we could see the initial breach and firing the line charges across the mine fields. And then the actual line charges blowing up and then the tanks going over them. And it was just real interesting to see how everything came together. All the coordination of all of the equipment that I got, you know, for them, see it all go to work finally.

The British came, when they were first coming over, they came to our supply which was the point of the initial defense, a part of Ripper. It was probably right around Manifah. They called us the speed pump battalion because we were the initial tip of the spear and the British came and got guidance as to how we did things. You know, little things like how we keep our water cool, where do we get our water.

Our unit was already deployed to Okinawa. We were scheduled to go over in August so we had done ARMOR, the standard Marine Corps evaluation test. So we were up to speed and everybody in our battalion has been together for over a year so we were, our battalion was basically ready for combat situation.

We didn't go into Kuwait City but you could see what the air war'd done and it was, it was really disruptive and I couldn't imagine being under the bombardment of the air. We had our chemical suits on. It was cool. Winter was cool there, but the oil could get on your skin. There was no way to wash it off. You were moving fast. We weren't taking prisoners or anything like that. The oil, it wasn't really that bad, but it was real dark. You couldn't see. Night maneuvers. We couldn't move at night. So thick and so black and so dark. NVGs wouldn't help.

Every driver had night vision goggles and you couldn't see from here five feet in front of you. It was like a black haze. Real thick black haze.

We had two people in our battalion get bit by scorpions but they were minor bites. They just required going to the BAS, being watched for a day and then released.

It started off slow. The supply system needed to catch up, because they were sending big stuff over at first and once repair parts didn't come as quickly as we expected it and a lot of the infantry stuff didn't come as quickly as we expected it, but once all the big stuff got over there it seemed like everything started falling in for the infantry and it worked pretty well. I was in charge of clothing our battalion and getting boots for everybody. We got as many boots as we wanted, you know, as many jungle boots as we wanted. The tan color boots we didn't get until four days going into the ground war which is, it was something they were trying to do and we understood that they didn't get them in time 'cause 20,000, they were trying to get over 20,000 pair of boots. They were lighter. They didn't have the steel shank in them at the bottom which would heat up.

There's little, on the sides, there's little eyelets that would pop out and sand would go inside your boots. Just the sand would eat up the soles.

We were mechanized. We had Amtracks. They were not really foot humpers. I forget what units were designated foot soldiers but foot marines, but we did little squad tactics and stuff like they did. I didn't. They did squad tactics and basically was working out of the Amtrack 'cause of the distance that you had to travel to get to someplace.

I would work with them and getting repair parts and they would go, they would take that, consolidate that from all the small units, go back to Jubayl, which is the supply base there and bring it up forward to us. We virtually could get whatever we wanted and some of it took time. Our battalion commander was happy once we finally went in. He was 100 percent sure that we had everything we needed to go in.

Just me as a supply man, seeing everything that I got come together and actually going to work. You know, you see, they always say, get this, get that, but you think, aw they don't really need that but once you get it for them you see it going to work and it makes you seem like you know what they need now.

I was the S4 supply and we used to go—in Manifah they had a desalinization plant there. It was kind of interesting to see how the—you know, how they could make 50,000 gallons of water. I believe it took a day, day and a half, and we just go down there, fill up our trucks and it would taste pretty good. It was—couldn't taste no salt at all. Once we went in to Kuwait City, you know, then we got back. We went down there to try to take a shower and get cleaned up and everything and it was shut down. The oil slick has just destroyed the whole little cove there at Manifah Bay.

It's going to take months, I guess, to clean up the oil. They had to truck water up from south. They moved the desalinization plant somewhere further south where it didn't get hit yet.

The Saudis couldn't believe it. You know, we didn't get to talk to many Saudis but we went to a store. There was a store there and we talked and they were real, they just couldn't believe what Saddam was doing. The main road from Kuwait City down to Khafji they dug up one lane, the northbound lane on it. I don't know if people knew that or not. It's just like they, there was just one lane open, the southbound lane was open, but they had to divide that in half so there's north and southbound lanes going from Kuwait City

You could see, as you come down you could see where the eight treads had tore up, you know 20mm cannons or 25mm cannons where they had shot the tanks. I had a lot of pictures, you know, of tanks laying there.

CRAIG A. FINN

Rank: Private First Class
Service: Marine Corps
Duty: Reconnaisance
Hometown: Newton, Illinois

Being in Reconnaissance, it was mostly our job just to observe and relay it back. We didn't get to see too much, but ours was just mostly information gathering. That's about all we did. At first it was kinda hard to get used to 'cause the sand being in everything, but, you know, after a while you got to adapt, you get used to it.

We was out by the second breach when one of the guys got blown out of a five-ton and I don't know, my emotions changed quite a bit when . . . you didn't really think about it until the rounds started coming in on you and then it's a whole different story. You just start thinking a whole different attitude about things.

We usually, you get scared like that and you pretty well lose everything so they kinda keep us lightheaded or, you know keep us from getting lightheaded so we know what's going on and what we're supposed to do so we don't forget our job. We had a lead element that was up in front of us and they was trying to get us through the breach. And they was right in the middle of it. We was back waiting for them to call us and then the rounds started coming in on them and they was adjusting them, so we started digging holes, started digging in.

It was tanks and LAIs shooting and TOWs and it just, you'd hear the shot and then whatever they hit was blown up. Most of them was bouncing across the ground 'cause it was out of range.

At first it was kinda neat 'cause we thought our guys was firing on the enemy, but they started getting closer and closer to the vehicles, you know, blowing up and it started getting scary for a while.

We got into Kuwait, we was supposed to be the eyes for the movement going up and we didn't get used too much for that. We was detached to Attack Force Grizzly some of us and we just used, a element, pulled security mostly. When they was cleaning up stuff, I personally didn't see any dead people, but the other platoons was cleaning up tanks and they did a BDA, that's a Battle Damage Assessment, coming back. And they got to see quite a bit of stuff.

We got to clear bunkers and stuff like that and you know you seen a little bit there. When we was going in to clear the bunkers, it was our job mostly just trying to see what as far as weapons and paperwork information stuff like that. And we were supposed to gather as much what we could but watch out for booby traps and that was about it on that. Our sergeant hit a. . . there was a line and he picked up something in there and he said the next thing he knew it popped and they got out of the bunker so it didn't harm them.

Those bunkers are made pretty good. It'd take a direct hit from, you know, RD round or something like that to take it out 'cause they're pretty fortified. They're dug in pretty good. We found a lot of ordnance and stuff, you know, ammo dumps, but other than that, bunkers was usually about a one-man hole, you know, enough to put a cot in and just walk around, just barely walk around. But that was for officers and just the non-rates and stuff like that they, they just had blankets on the ground and they pretty well, they had a little bit of room in there.

It has a hole for a exit, you know, just a walkway and it was sandbagged all the way around it. And had boards over the top with sandbags to fortify it even more. I'd say it was around six feet deep with a roof on it. There wasn't a whole lot of room to move around in.

As far as we got is Al-Jabar and then they pulled us off and we were regrouped with our unit and we went in to, we was going through the outskirts of Kuwait City and Kuwaiti International Airport. And we seen the tanks that had been blown up from our guys, but we didn't get to go through and look at the buildings too much.

Their tanks—as far as I don't know what kind of ammunition hit them—but the whole turret was off of them. They was just shredded, it looked like somebody just left it out there and let it rust for a long time.

As far as dying, you know, I was real scared before and now, you know, it just kinda takes you down to reality and shows what could really happen to you. All the other marines that died. So it doesn't make you as scared as what you was before.

RENEE M. LEBLANC

Rank: Private First Class
Service: Army
Duty: Combat Medical Specialist
Home State: New Hampshire

I been over here since June of last year. And I'll leave in June of '92. We've been over here like, our company, 583rd Medical Company. We're an ambulance unit and we've been working over here since about December and in January we actually came to Tent City and we were working out of the tents. We'd get called for runs. And a run consists of a bus or an ambulance and they have 66 Mercedes pack buses and like they accommodate 12 litters or as many ambulatory as we can put on the bus. And we bring the medical patients to like the designated hospitals here in Germany. And we bring them there when they're coming back from Saudi if they're injured casualties.

They get, like when they first started coming back before when people were like injured like mostly the football injuries like you hear on TV, just the little stuff. There wasn't, I mean there wasn't anything coming back that was serious like broken legs, broken arms, like something else came back. You know, pregnant. We dealt with that. And now like when the war did like first start like two weeks we didn't do any work 'cause they weren't sending any planes out.

I haven't dealt with any of the American POWs. Right now we're dealing with real like casualties. 'Cause they coming in. The other day we had someone like on a cardiac system and we had, oh the other day Mass like you be talking to him, like he had a guy like with tubes and he had catheters and like you go into the ASF down by the fight line that's where the patients come off the front line and if you go in there sometimes you can see like people with amputated like legs and stuff. I mean, I haven't myself seen anybody but I just hear what comes back to me.

I got trained at Fort Sam Houston, in Texas. I'm a 91, I'm a combat, well my MOS is a Combat Medical Specialist. I have been trained during the training at Fort Sam for that 91 alpha. My MOS while I was down there, I got trained for EMT, I'm EMT qualified, and I'm CPR qualified.

The casualties pretty much have to be stabilized before they come here. We transport them to the four different hospitals. We transport them, like, they have to be pretty much stable and they have to, you know, if they're not stable they've gotta stay at the ASF or they have ambulances and they run them priority, 'cause the ambulances are like a bit faster than the buses and you know they can get through traffic a lot better than the buses. And if they're priority they either like a helicopter'll come in. If they want to bring them any distance, they bring in a 'copter.

Just yesterday I guess there was a 'copter coming in to go pick up somebody. So I haven't ridden with anybody and I haven't heard of anybody riding with anybody. But yesterday they were supposed to have somebody ride in the helicopter to bring him to the hospital.

They're glad to be back, I mean, even though they're injured they worry about their personal belongings, you know, they've got a good frame of mind. I mean, you know, some people, like we've got some psych patients.

You know we get like the battle fatigue, like the people who've been out there for a while. We get them back, too, also. Battle fatigue is like, uh, God, it's like somebody's been out there for a while. It just like, they can't, they've dealt with as much as they can out there and they just like, the desert or whatever, it just, they can't deal with it anymore and it just gets, like they've had enough of it. And they're not coming back.

And they'll be like, oh, one patient I had, he was just like there worried, like one patient was worried how long it took to get to the hospital and if we're going to make it there and if I was a medic, like I was a driver at the time 'cause I also drove the buses too. And when I was driving he was like, "Are you a medic? Do you know what you're doing? Do you know how to drive this bus?" They just ask a lot of questions. They're just really unsure and you know some of them are just a hypochondriac. You know, they're, they just worry a lot.

They're all ages, too. Pretty much like from like 23 to any age. I'd say about 45. You know it's a pretty midrange. I have, I've seen like officers come back, I've seen regular enlisted come back. It's a wide range.

I wanted to do this kind of work for long time. My stepmother's a physical therapist. She's in the medical field. My grandmother's kind of in the medical field and my courses in high school were all like science-oriented, math-oriented, and I do good in math and I always have. I'm interested, like I wanted to be a physical therapist and my stepmother helped me choose my courses for like high school. I still want to go to college, but the problem to me was like I didn't have the money, my parents didn't have the money. You know, I hadn't saved very much like throughout my life.

I was in business, back in New Hampshire, managing

in a department store and I just wanted to make sure that I had, you know, if I wanted to be in business or if I wanted to go into the medical field. And I said I might as well. I'm still young. I'll go into the Army, they can give me the education, they can get me started and give me, you know they have a GI bill which is going to help me out and I can go to college when I get back.

JOHN CONNORS

Rank: Colonel
Service: Marine Corps
Duty: Mobilization Administration
Hometown: Newbury Park, California

I am system engineer with UNISYS Corporation, air defense systems. The unit that I'm the OIC, the Mobilization Processing Center, was called up to take care of the Selected Marine Corps Reserve units that were activated. Just as a way of overview, within the Marine Corps they have stations of initial assignment. These are bases around the country that mobilize reserve units to which go to be processed either units or individual reservists, and so Camp LeJeune, North Carolina, and Camp Pendleton were designated in a mobilization plan as stations of initial assignments. Both of those were activated, so our reserve unit was activated to take care of the Selected Marine Corps Reserve units called up.

There are actually more units in the plan, but only two got activated so all of the marines' reservists went either through Camp Pendelton, California, or Camp LeJeune, North Carolina. In the presidential callup, the 200K, all the units were Selected Marine Corps units or detachments, people having a particular skill that was needed to reinforce the active side and so we processed, I'd say maybe about seven to nine thousand, I forgot the split on the Selected Marine Corp Reserve units. As soon as the president got approval from Congress on a partial mobilization and I think the date was 26 January, I was just looking at it the other day, that's when the individual

Ready Reservists were called up. Now these are individuals that have obligated service but are not associated with a reserve unit.

And so the call out, they have a procedure which they do. They run a tape which has everybody's name on it and they generate orders and they're sent to their home and then these marines have to execute these orders and these are the individuals that responded in mass not only the Marine Corps side now, but I'm sure in the other services, with very little notice. I mean they had to report within one or two days and to tie up your personal affairs in that amount of time—in most cases it was left to the wife or family or something. So these individuals started coming in en masse and these individuals went into replacement pools, combat replacement companies, and the purpose for these was in the event there was—instead of a one-sided war—a more even one, and there were going to be casualties, mass casualties, there would be in place trained replacement people to fill in, and so we were in the process of training these individual Ready Reservists into combat replacement companies, and then these companies, 250 each, would go over and some had already gone into Saudi to be in place. Because it only went 100 hours our iteration of this training cycle soon stopped and then we were sending people home.

What we never realized was, and we had read many times that at Camp Pendleton we could get up to 14,000 people in the first 50 days. Well, you can talk about that, but until you see masses like 5,000 coming at you, 500 a day, you don't anticipate the logistics requiring in getting a rack for each marine and the sheets and the blankets and opening up other mess halls and opening other camps. And the impact across the whole staff functionings, not just us doing the processing and the training but across the whole base. We had to jump some loops on a continuous basis.

We always thought that we could do the mission, but we were dependent upon some additional support. These were additional bodies coming in that are either pre-assigned or going to the base here and getting personnel support. And we had to work both ends of that because for purposes of our normal once-a-month training we only have a core of individuals who are trained. We don't come and practice this every month. So to come up to speed and get the number of bodies that are needed to do this required going to base and required bringing some other people on active duty. So what you have, in effect, you have an organization that's being created—at the same time you're trying to do what your mission is you're creating this organization in order to do the mission—and it's somewhat difficult but I think we did a good job doing it.

Now we have to reverse the whole process. In fact, we have been into that planning process. A number of people are doing that; we presently have teams that will be going into Saudi Arabia. We have marines in Hawaii and also on Okinawa. These are reservists who are taking over the missions of the regular side of the house and we will be sending some teams there to do some advance administrative processing. There is quite an administrative burden outprocessing people. You have to create a form that records their active duty time—it's called a DD2-14. You have to determine the date that they will leave. You have to do the final settlement of pay and it's not so much body intensive as very paper intensive.

Pay has to be addressed, too. In a situation of coming into mobilization and having a system in place that can respond effectively and quickly to the number of people that are being processed into it. So that the individual marine or serviceman is not, does not bear the brunt of a system that can't accommodate these, they should not suffer and have a cash flow problem because of a system problem in the military. That's my personal opinion. I think it's shared by a lot of people.

When they come in, they get an advance payment of 80 percent of one month's pay. The Soldiers and Sailors Relief Act allows them if they have any loans to, the loan will go down at least to six percent, some lenders have even gone to zero during this time they're on active duty. If they have contracts they can get out of rental agreements and stuff. There's a number of things. But in a lot of cases the individuals make more on the civilian side than they do on the reserve side just by virtue of their rank. And time and service. And so it's a financial burden to the family and I think that goes all across the, not just the Marine Corps, all services. You take pilots making, you know, close to 100,000 dollars or whatever and their house payment may be, you know, 2,000, 3,000, 4,000 dollars. Well, they're not making that kind of money as a pilot in the service.

And, on a lower scale, the same is true with some enlisted people. So I don't know what can be done. What needs to be done in my mind is a mechanism that whatever the marine is rated, that he gets it in timely fashion. That he does not suffer the consequences of some kind of automated system that can't respond and get him his money when it's owed to him on time. I think in most cases it was done. Most of them made out allotments to the families which went home, but allotment takes 30 days to get activated in the system and here we had a war that ended before many of them, you know, had the allotment processed.

We are presently doing after-action reports. We're taking a look at our wartime TO, that's Table of Organization, for this particular base. The TO documents the number of bodies that are needed to support this mission if this crisis were to happen again and we already know that we need to structure—here at Pendleton they created a warrior training command which did two, well, essentially three functions: it processed all the mobilized marines, a big consolidated administrative organization which came under headquarters and support battalion, service battalion, but there was another thing we didn't realize was the administrative burden that we would have and then the third mission was doing the training. We have to by law put people who have not been in combat arms through a refresher training and our course was about fourteen days. Refresher to their combat arms and to some patrolling and some other courses.

It was the base's responsibility under this warrior training command and a colonel who is the C.O. of the Reserves Support unit was dual hatted as the commanding officer of warrior training command.

A lot of reservists made real sacrifices. You know, civilian doctor's insurance is unbelievable and for them to come on active duty and even if they're trying to maintain the practice on the outside if they're close enough to do something on the weekend you still have those insurance payments. I will say from my perspective there was a great willingness for those reserve doctors and dentists to come in and support and be right beside us working some long, long hours. We were running 16 hours a day in some cases, seven days a week. And we finally on the outprocessing we're now gearing up to having two shifts. We'll go a good 16 hours, maybe a little longer, but it won't be the same people going the 16 hours daily. And that's one of the problems when you go into this with limited resources personnel, that means everybody just tightens up a little and goes longer and here at this base we have said from day one and I've said it to all my people, that we are in the business of servicing mobilized reserves.

That is our whole mission in life to treat those marines the same way we want to be treated if we were coming through the front gate and so we tried to accommodate them, accommodate them and process them in an efficient way and with minimum impact to them, leaving them maximum amount of time for training for them. You know, this is administrative, they had to go through medical screening, dental screening, and I.D. tags and dog tags and a number of other things, but we tried to get as efficient as possible so that we would minimum the impact on training.

And then they would get into, if they were a regular unit, they went immediately over to the FMF side of the house and joined up with a regular active unit, and then as soon as transportation was lined up they would be getting out of country, out of CONUS rather. There's a dependency upon the reserve side of the house for combat service and even some of the combat arms, and I think just for budget reasons it's going to, there's going to be some reductions later on which puts more missions on the reserve side of the house.

JAMES KESSOCK

Rank: Staff Sergeant
Service: Army
Duty: Civil Engineering
Hometown: St. Claire, Pennsylvania

I'm originally a carpenter. While we were working, we had a lot of people—there wasn't many people at that time who used to come and scrounge a lot of wood for us. And we kind of got tired, because people, they'd say we couldn't give them wood and not try to help them out with little scraps, you know, because they wanted to build something for their camp. So I came up with an idea to my commander, and I said, hey, why don't we come up with a little self-help store? And he said, "What do you mean?" What it was meant to be was to let people build little projects for their camp and make it feel like home, because everybody wanted to have little drawers or something for their clothes and their food and stuff.

When we first came up, like I said, they kind of looked at me like I was strange, but they finally said, okay, let's go with it, because people need—instead of going to supply downtown which would have cost a lot of money, let's see what happens. So we came up with a little thing where we would order for squadrons, we would order the wood for them, but for the other people what we would do is, we made up our own plan, that would be nice and comfortable over their cot, bunk, we would build little bookshelves, little wardrobes, little end tables, stuff like that.

And at first when we started we weren't big, we just had a couple of saws, and we would recut strips. And they would cut everything else. And as we got bigger and better we ordered, you know, bigger saws and bigger things, because we got so popular that we couldn't—we only got, like, forty or fifty people out a day. So I suggested that we get bigger saws and just precut everything. So if they wanted to build a table, we would say, what number do you want, and they would come in, I want number two, I want number three.

Then we cut strips, and like I said, before, they would cut it themselves, cross-cut them. I would cut them in regular 12, 16, 24 strips. And then as we got along and bigger, we'd precut everything. It was just like coming into the store and saying, hey, I want to build that, and everything was precut to size and all they had to do was put it together. And we got up to 120, 140 people out a day. And we would service about 300 people a day to the store, but we just had people come in there. The commander loved it. In fact, during the war, we shut it down for two weeks. And during the war, I couldn't believe how people wanted it. They wanted the store open. So what happened, even during the war we finally opened it up, because it kept the people's minds not on the war, but going, you know, still alert, but to keep their minds occupied

This is in Saudi Arabia, and we built the largest tent city in the world. And people, like I said, people will come in, because we were on all different shows, the Today Show, Good Morning America, they did a little—and the history, war history from the Pentagon, and they took pictures, too. It was one of the biggest morale—well, they said it was going to be one of the biggest morale boosters in any kind of war.

I was there when Bob Hope came over. Oh, man, I'll tell you, it really boosted me, I wanted to see him for how many years, you know, and to see him personally just was a thrill, and it did, ever since—especially on Christmas. We had been hearing that a lot of people were coming, and I guess—we weren't really front line, you know, they basically were going toward the front lines, because I can understand that. And we were all saying, oh, they're not going to see us, because we're in between everything and they're going to go to the bigger bases and where the, you know, where the bigger brass and all that. But then when he came there, I mean, everybody was just excited. And it came out to be really good.

And after that, and then they started getting a little bit looser, you know, we were worried about our work, but we also had a time to enjoy ourselves a little bit. And we tried to come up with little things that the people would do. But like I said, the biggest thing on that is just since I came down, and they looked at it and they wanted all the other bases to come up with some kind of stuff, and they said they want this in the war.

I came up with the idea, and like I said, I just—to me, inside, it's always got to be inside of me, that it might not be my name anywhere else, but I know that I did something for people for just—to make Sand City a little bit better.

I just want to say one thing, that the people that worked with us, the six original people that came, we started with six people, and we had to come up to almost 12 people to help us out in the store, and everyone of them was great. We worked together really well.

In the beginning we went in groups, you know, so I'd say we built close to 200, 250. And then, you know, that has some part to do with it. But basically everybody, it was a team effort. What happened is, you know, we were only so many people. Everbody thought it was our job, you know. Civil engineers are going to do everything. But what happened is, when we first come, the maintenance people were there, too, but their planes weren't there. And they helped us out a lot. What they would do is they would send us 100 people a night, and they would say, okay, like, they'd pick me and ten other CE people and they'd say, I want you to take ten guys and go out—and we'd go out there and knock out ten, 15 tents, during a four-hour span, you know.

These tents were approximately 32x16 feet. 32x20 feet. We got to where some would house, you know, anywhere from eight to 12. Well, at first, eight to 16 people, up to 16 people, and then as we got more tents, the average was about 12 people per tent. So it was pretty crowded, but that's why these projects that we built really came in handy, because it separated everybody else, and everybody had something to put their stuff in, and it made it a lot neater. It was like little rooms, you know. But it became a big thing. Good Morning America and everything.

It's bizarre, it's also bizarre to be in a war and to see a little self-help store. A self-help store in the desert? Who would know?

The biggest thing on the Today Show, Willard Scott came to see our store, because that was one of, like I said, he would go to the bigger highlights areas, like the flight lines and the chow hall and the self-help store, and so we were opening among them as one of the biggest things for him to come, and since we got a lot of patrons there. But he came in, and we built a chair for him, and engraved our organizations and who built it. And we were afraid it wasn't big enough for him, because Willard Scott's a big person. But he came in and he just loved it. So after he did his show, and we did a little thing on the Today Show, after the show was over he came over and he liked the chair so much he said he wanted to break it down so that he could take it back, and I understand now he, back in the studio when he does the weather in the studio that he sits in his chair and does it from there. So it was one of the chairs that we had on show for people to build, too.

DOUGLAS W. HOPLER

Rank: Sergeant
Service: Air Force
Duty: Base Supply
Hometown: Freiburg, Maine

I got to Saudi Arabia on Thanksgiving Day. I arrived in Jedda, Saudi Arabia. We had it pretty easy compared to most of the people down there. I work in base supply. I run their computer system. I just run their system that they use to keep track of parts and things that they need for the aircraft and what-not and various things on base vehicles or whatever. My role was just to try to make sure that the computer was up as much as it could be. For the whole base—just various aircraft, vehicles, anything. Office supplies, anything that they needed.

When they put in a requisition, depending on the severity of it, I would say it took an average of one month or two, probably. But for the really important things—aircraft and getting parts for them—it was really quick. Three or four days.

The thing I remember most is the night that the B-52s landed at our base after their first bombing. When the first plane touched down, a lot of the bomber maintenance people were outside. And we were outside of our hangar—that's where base supply was; it was an aircraft hangar. And when they touched down, a bunch of tension was relieved, kind of. You know, everybody was hurraying and "It's started." You know, we want to get home; we want to get on with our lives. And we thought this was going to be the first step toward that. It was an odd feeling watching them land.

KEVIN BRATTON

Rank: Specialist
Service: Army
Duty: Airborne
Hometown: Castro Valley, California

I'm from Castro Valley, California. It's about two miles south of Oakland, in the Bay Area. Well, the situation and things I came across, basically, living and dealing with people was the biggest thing over there, because everyone has the time that — you know, they get low points and you've got to accept that, and even if you're at your low point, you learn to accept those people. And we were pretty much working with reservists later in January, and a couple of points that came to my mind and still stick there is that they're getting there in January and we're working with them, and some of them were complaining they missed Christmas and they gotta do this and stuff. And then we're looking around at all the people that got here, you know, we were in the first two packs over on August 8th. And they're just, you know, pouting around and whining like, and you're just wondering what's going to go on if we do have to go in, something like that.

And we found ourselves, you know, just saying, "Hey, keep quiet," I guess. It hit them when we started getting contact on patrols at night, and because they were driving us out to ambush sites, and once they started seeing that, they realized—then I noticed a lot of attitudes changed.

I believed, when we were going in, we would see more retaliation from them, because our units, the one I'm with, we went down to Panama, you know. And we considered that they were going to retaliate, and we walked in and they walked out. It was that simple.

When you're in the foxhole, it's usually out in the perimeter in front of where we sleep, and we go on guard shifts out there. And when we go to sleep and eat and stuff like that, they cover for us after our shifts, and we go behind, usually a hill, for cover and concealment. And that's usually when we eat. And everytime you eat, you have to dig a hole and bury, and then you've got to burn trash, your garbage. And basically, when you're in the foxhole, you don't sleep, you're primarily, you know, you're not supposed to be looking through your sights, but you're supposed to be up and around, night-vision goggles or whatever it may be.

Considering where we were, in the desert, surprisingly we — we didn't have hot showers, but we were able to take showers. They had a water system hooked up in the TAA. And meals, basically we had — the last week we were out there before we went in, we had hot meals once a day. And that was for lunch. Other than that, it's been the MREs we had for meals.

Our unit, we were the lead unit going in on G Minus 1. And when we were going in, we had SIOPS, and what we do, before we start with artillery, the infantry starts small arms and stuff like that, the SIOPS go on a vehicle that is up with the armor, and what they do, they tell, they stick in Arabic and tell them, surrender, you will not die, drop your rifles, put your hands up in the air. And they heard that, and they did exactly as they were told. So we called off the press and there was no artillery fired. I mean, on the initial movement.

The lower enlisted was very poor looking, hungry. Some of the officers, they looked pretty well fed. That's basically how it was. Same with clothing. The lower enlisted, it wasn't too good for them. Some were wearing normal boots, like we'd buy in a store type, and some were in military, and those were pretty damaged. I'd say on average in our company, we used three pair of boots. Because we got new boots when we got in the country, and we wore them out, and you turn in an old pair, and they give you new ones. I'm on my third pair of boots. It's the walking on the rocks and sand, and the weather basically, too.

In August it was quite warm, very warm. And then we were in the winter time, in December, and it got cold. The weather was pretty clear, though, basically. At night, I'd say it dropped down into the twenties. And during the day with the wind chill, I'd say it dropped down to about fifty, fifty-five.

Going in, truthfully, I was hoping that our intel was right, that they wouldn't be fighting. Basically, they had a feeling that most of them would be fighting, but most of them would only be fighting because there was one guy in charge, and they'd be shot. And as we came across the lines, we had seen a lot of officers shot in the back, and intelligence confirmed that they had been shot by their own people, and then they surrendered. We didn't shoot no small arms, but found dead with small arms weaponry. And it was not chest wounds, it was in the head. I mean, point-blank type thing. And those are — you know, you're just looking at — and the big thing was, when you were walking through, and the EPWs had already walked by you, you're looking at their positions, you're thinking if they would have stood there and fought, they would have done a lot more damage than they thought.

We brought the dead to like casualty collection points. And pretty much we just kept going. We were the lead element. And so as we got by the EPWs and made sure they were strip-searched, and then we let them go by and walk and a rear detachment took care of them. We kept going.

It was weird, when we were coming out, what was kind of weird, we had the feeling, when we were walking by them, you could see them waving and throwing kisses at us. I was just amazed at what they were doing, and they were shaking our hands. And these are the Iraqi soldiers. And they were shaking our hands.

They—I think if they were fed properly, you know, and kept in intelligence, they would have fought, but right now, some of the soldiers up there, the Iraqis, don't know the war's over. It's just—we talked to one lieutenant of a platoon, and the last time they had got fed was—we had a box of food, and that came two weeks ago. So officers pretty much fend for themselves.

We worked with some coalition troops, too. What we did, our battalion commanders, they swapped with the French team for platoon. They sent some platoon over to us, and we sent a platoon to the French. We traded MREs, type of stuff like that. They're not bad. From what I can see and what I've been told and I've read, they're . . . well, their history as a military speaks for itself.

They were telling us everything, from political moves all the way down to us. Whatever our commander knows, he relays down to the commander and all the way down to the lowest ranking troops. And our troops are told everything, from the intelligence to—I mean, they were briefed thoroughly, every day, so we had a good idea what's going on, and who's where and what.

ROBERT WOLFERTZ

Rank: Lieutenant Colonel
Service: Marine Corps
Duty: Executive Officer
Hometown: Windham, New Hampshire

I went over with the offload control group for Maritime Prepositioning Ships Squadron 3 and when that was done I was slated to be a battalion commander. The incumbent is a selected colonel. We were expecting him to get promoted the first of October so I could take the battalion. It never happened so I wound up being the ExO for my unit. It kind of got put together for the operation. We had two battalions and then picked up a third one none of which were indigenous. We two regular battalions and then a reserve battalion from New England.

It was fairly well organized. We established a tent city in a place called Ras-el-Gar initially and then once we started to move north we were used to living in the field. And we got more used to living in the field and we just continued displacing more until we finally made our way up to the border and then into Kuwait.

Until we actually got into the ground combat operations, we were getting a hot meal for breakfast, a hot meal for supper and an MRE for lunch. We wound up using our what's called a Sanitor, an NBC decontamination unit as a shower unit. And we practiced setting that unit up in case of we might actually have to become involved in decon and we used that for showers so we got a shower well, not real often, but often enough that it felt good.

When I was still with Third Marines initially we did a whole lot of cross training with Saudi marines at Ras-el-Gar and then the Third Marine Regiment went on to do a whole lot more training as events unfolded and in fact wound up assisting the Saudis and Qataris in the battle of Khafji.

We had to do a mine breaching operation in conjunction with the ground offensive operation. And in fact we had anticipated that we would have to go through one obstacle belt. It wound up being two. The obstacles and the mines were—there were lots of them there. The wind had blown a lot of sand away so they were exposed which made it fairly easy.

The first obstacle belt that we went through we knew they were there because we had a bunch of Iraqi prisoners of war who surrendered and then volunteered to go back and show us the clear lane through the first obstacle belt. They didn't know the lane through the second obstacle belt so we actually wound up doing a night assault breach using the engineers and they blew lanes into the mine field. There were plenty of mines. I've got pictures. You could see them on both sides of the breach forever and ever. And they had these plastic boxes. They looked like a very large briefcase that the mines came in and when we found—our regiment went on to take Al-Jabar Air Field and there were thousands of those mine boxes, empty mines boxes just laying all over the place.

The obstacle belts that we went through were very well planned and laid out. The defenses themselves I was expecting a lot more out of their fortifications. They made good use of the wire. There were a lot of mines there, a lot of obstacles, but the actual fortifications and defensive positions behind those as much time as they had there I expected to see a lot more than we really did.

First Battalion Twenty-fifth Marines was the EPW handling battalion. We had anticipated that there would be a large number of prisoners of war and we started taking them. They were complacent, humble and in some cases genuinely glad to see us. I mean, I saw people, you know, they looked at us and they were just smiling. I heard one interesting story. You may have heard this one already about this. First Battalion Twenty-fifth Marines participated in this one. There was one Iraqi soldier who stood up with a UCLA sweatshirt on waving his arms. And I think he had 64 other people who wanted to surrender. This guy had—it was a UCLA student who was home in Iraq when the war broke out, was drafted, and then thrown in where he didn't want to be and we came through and he said, you know, "Hey I've been waiting for you guys a long time and I've got 64 others with me."

We used a couple of shortwave radios and got the BBC all the time. The BBC provided a good update for us. We combined that with our intelligence reports and we had a pretty good idea what was going on.

Probably, for me, one of the two most gratifying things about the—obviously the most gratifying thing is that it was so short and we took so few casualties. The other thing was to recognize the support that we got from the folks back home. I received letters from people that I hadn't heard from in some cases 20 years. From all over the United States. Alaska, Florida, North Carolina and the theme was always the same, about the support that we were getting. And I heard about the yellow ribbons and the flags and the pro support marches. Having been around during the Vietnam era, it was just a, I looked at this as what a tremendous healing this was for our country since that time and I walked in here and saw it all and I really, it got me when I walked in here.

I had a critical MOS as an enlisted marine and I never got to go fight in Vietnam. I got out of the Marines, I enlisted in 1966, got out in 1969 and went back to college in the middle of the height of the antiwar protests and I was really, I was just shocked. I had heard about what was going on and I was just shocked to see the total lack of understanding of the commitment that the U.S. military personnel had made and the way they were treated for decisions that they didn't make. And then to see the way the country responded to support us this time again I—to me it just, I just, my sense is that there's been a tremendous healing.

I got a, I received a letter from an old friend who was an avid antiwar protester during the Vietnam era. Her husband was a draft dodger, she helped him evade the draft. I got a letter from her. In fact I was in Kuwait. We were in the thick of things when I got this letter and she related how wrong she had been and how if she had it all to do over again she might still not have supported the cause, but she would not have turned her back on the troops the way she did and wound up thanking all of us brave guys over here doing the job. I'm not sure all of us were brave guys, but we were there and she recognized that and it was really for me just an indication of the healing of the open wound that has been Vietnam in our country, the healing of that wound, and I really feel good for that.

I feel that a lot of people made a big sacrifice for this response. But I think that the reservists made the biggest sacrifice of all. Because they did, you know a lot of the guys from New England as you well know are individualistic and a lot of them were self-employed. So whereas the reservists who had a job that was guaranteed because they were employed by somebody else, you know guaranteed under the Soldiers and Sailors Relief Act. They have a lot of self-employed people who don't have those guarantees and yet they were there doing the job and boy my hat's off to those guys. They really deserve a lot of credit.

I think it's important historically to note that because of the mission that we had, which was to secure the First Marine Division's left flank, and because we were foot mobile infantry, and because the First Marine Division's main effort was a mech armor attack through a major obstacle belt, in order for that mech armor attack to occur, both of the Division's flanks had to be secured. Because we were foot mobile infantry and could not move as fast as the mech armor task force, we were actually infiltrated into Kuwait and we were there 48 hours before the actual ground offensive kicked off.

The two obstacle belts that we attacked were defended. The resistance was light, but most of it was supporting arms fire that was not very effective. In the regiment we had, let's see, about 2,200 men. I guess probably the most, for me, the two most interesting aspects of that were listening to the BBC, hearing about, you know, the U.S. forces getting ready to commence the ground offensive at any time now or the coalition forces getting ready to and we were already there.

And the second part was just a really amazing phenomenon occurred as we rolled in. The night that we actually conducted our breach, the weather was coming out of the north from the Iraqis' back, blowing wind and rain from their back toward our faces. Which means it masked our movement. They couldn't hear us coming. We conducted the breach and it got to be warning time, we'd passed through, the wind shifted, the clouds went away. The winds started coming from the south from our backs, blew the clouds away, the sun came out so we could, we were able to call air and artillery on observed targets.

It was absolutely the most amazing thing I've ever experienced. The wind was with us going in because it masked our movement, it covered our noise. And when we got in, the wind came from our backs, blowing the clouds away from the Iraqis, letting the airplanes be able to see and for our observers to mark for supporting arms fire. It was just incredible.

The battalions did call in supporting arms strikes. Another factor needs to be brought out. We had, you asked me earlier if we had coalition forces with us and I said, no, and that's true we didn't, except that each of the units had a couple of Kuwaiti interpreters with us. They helped out tremendously. And in this particular instance we had an Army SIOPS detachment with us. And what those guys did is that night, in fact, two nights before we called in some heavy duty air and artillery strikes and then the SIOPS folks go up and start broadcasting, telling these guys to surrender or it's going to get worse. And they actually wound, we started taking EPWs before the kickoff of the official ground offensive.

One of the most impressive feelings of my life was the, I guess it was the morning before the official ground offensive, we had a B-52 strike on the, on the obstacle belt, or near the obstacle belt that we had to breach and you could literally feel, we were at that point, oh shoot, the regimental CP was probably 12 klicks back from the obstacle belt, the battalions were forward. And 12 klicks back you could feel the ground shake from the B-52 strike. It was just incredible.

I think that that's part of the reason that we got such little resistance on the ground as we did. It wasn't a matter of nobody left, there were definitely people there, but there was not a, they weren't determined to stay. And obviously if you just had the crap kicked out of you with bombing for a month and then all of a sudden you hear and I know that they heard, we found radios in those guys' possessions, commercial radios, that they listened to the BBC, too. And they knew that we were coming and knew it was going to be a big force. And they said, "Whoa, it ain't worth this!"

If you look around this building you'll see a lot of signs that say Task Force Ripper. Task Force Ripper was a mechanized armor task force—heavy tank assets, AAVs—assault amphibian vehicles—that we used like the Army has APCs, just a large force that was the Division's main effort. As I said, we had a regiment on either side that secured the flanks. That task force along with another one centered around a Marine Regiment which was also a mech armor task force called Papa Bear. They actually went through the breach. Ripper was the heavier of the forces after they came from the south to the north, south of the Brecon oil fields, and then swung to the northwest, rolled past Al-Jabar Air Field and eventually right on up into the airport. Papa Bear swung to the right initially, secured the right flank above another Marine Regiment and went back through the oil field and assisted sweeping north up toward the airport also. Those guys I know having spoken to their executive officers that they wound up just bypassing tremendous enemy armor forces that just crumbled, you know, T-72 tanks with guys standing on the turrets: "We give up." The Marines said, "Okay," pointed in the direction to go south and just rolled on by.

They did a lot of shooting and destroyed a lot of tanks, but once the Iraqis started giving up, just pointed them in the direction to surrender and that's what they did. The

T-72 was the, is Russia's premier tank. We didn't actually face those as foot mobile infantry, the mech armor guys did, but in talking with them, they were not impressed with the Iraqis' ability to use those, to use the tank for what it's capability probably is. They just, they weren't good at gunnery. They missed a lot of shots. They didn't take very many shots and absolutely no will to hang in there.

As soon as they started taking any fire from us, it was, "Okay, we give up." I guess one other thing that I'm not sure anyone is aware of, the night after we made that breach, the next night we started an attack on Al-Jabar Air Field which had been, there had been a corps, an Iraqi corps headquarters located there so it was heavily, it had been heavily defended. And the night that we went in there, it literally rained oil. It just got, in the afternoon, it just got as black as night and all night long it just came down. If I could conceal my uniform, the little black spots, it just kept coming down. The next day the sun came out for a while and then it rolled back in and for three days all we had was like it was nighttime for three solid days, just a thick black oil cloud.

In fact, one of the things that has happened since then is that those of us who were there have had entries made in our health records that we did, that we were in this kind of an atmosphere for as long a time as we were. Hopefully, it's not going to turn out to be the Agent Orange of the Iraqi war. You know, "Agent Oil." But it was pretty nasty.

Yesterday when we were coming back, we had our division support area established at a place called Manifah Bay so we would up coming down to Al Jubay, south. We backtracked over a lot of the ground that we had initially defended, prepared defenses for and that ground had been stark and barren, no sign of life whatsoever and yesterday as we came back down, there were like nomadic tribes, groups of people, just interspersed all along the highway, waving their arms, yelling at us, cheering, waving flags. And the one that really got me is along with seeing a lot of Saudi and Kuwaiti flags here was some kid with a home-made American flag. He was waving this American flag back and forth. I just—wow!

It was like a, just a big, a piece of a sheet and he had colored in the blue, the stars weren't right, but he had blue with stars and red and white stripes, and it was very evidently an American flag. And here was this kid waving it back and forth. And you know I just really felt good about it, I wondered what kind of a response we were going to get once this thing was over. You know, if the Arabs were just going to "Okay, you did it, now go." And it's not that way at all.

I think probably the initial euphoria of the victory is still there and they're really glad that we came. My instincts tell me that they probably don't want us there for a long term presence, but I guess it depends on what happens in that portion of the world. They obviously couldn't have done it by themselves, they might have made a good stab at it and they did a lot of good stuff that I am aware of in the fighting, but we provided the biggest backing and I don't think it would have turned out the same if we hadn't been there. I guess I was concerned that I might see the same kind of response there that we got during Vietnam and it wasn't, it was people who were genuinely glad for us being there and I mean, I'm talking, you have to understand, that this is out in the middle of nowhere that these people are lined up along this highway.

This is 50-60 miles north of Al Jubay which is the only

major city on the coast from Khafji down to Dhahran. You get to Al Jubay and it's the first city and we're not talking Heresford, PA, or anything, it's fairly big but here are all these people lined up along the road just waving and cheering. Not even knowing when troops are going to be coming out.

This is in Saudi Arabia, no mining at all. Coming out of Kuwait the destruction was incredible. We came down along the coastal road, in fact, I told you we were the first regiment in, we were the last regiment out, too. There are a lot of craters from the bombs. What I saw coming on the road coming out of Kuwait, the coastal road, was how the Iraqis had chopped it all up and then how—we caught them in convoys on that road a number of times and you can just, I mean I saw a tank that had been hit and it looked like what happened is that the turret went up in the air and came down and landed right back on the tank, upside down.

And there were scenes of destruction like that all the way from Kuwait City down to the border. And a lot of places where the Rockeye hit and you'd see a whole bunch of pockmarks in a road. A couple of places where the big craters in the road that had been filled in. And the closer we got to the Saudi/Kuwaiti border, the Iraqis chopped one of the roads—in fact, they chopped both the roads all up. It was a dual highway and they just took one of the lanes or one of the sectors of it and just completely destroyed it. And the other one they cut back and forth like a, like to stop terrorists from coming in.

Another gratifying thing to see was, we came across remains, burned-up Iraqis in tanks and our guys took the time to pull them out, bury them, and mark the spot, and then we forwarded the exact grid locations back up the chain so they can be eventually be recovered. What we did was just forward the information as to where they were located and sent that back up our chain so it could be delivered to the Saudis and they'll do whatever they have to for the Iraqis to get the remains back where they belong if that's what they choose to do.

Glossary

AAV—Assault Amphibious Vehicle

ADA—Air Defense Artillery

AM—Amplitude Modulation

APC—Armored Personnel Carrier

ASF—Aviation Support Facility

AWS—Amphibious Warfare School

BAS—Battle Assistance Station

BD—Iraqi armor: Air Portable Fire Support Vehicle

BDRM—Iraqi armor: Reconnaissance Vehicle

BMP—Iraqi armor: Armored Personnel Carrier

CAG—Carrier Airwing Commander

CONUS—Continental United States

CP—Command Post

CRC—Combat Replacement Company

CVC—Cut "V" (Dodge Blazer)

EOD—Explosive Ordnance Disposal

EMT—Emergency Medical Treatment

EPW—Enemy Prisoner of War

EW—Electronic Warfare

FDC—Fire Detection Center

FMF—Fleet Marine Force

FRI—Fire Radar Image

FTC—Fleet Training Center

Frago—Situational Order

Frog—CH-46 (helicopter)

GCI—Ground Control Intercept

H&S—Headquarters and Supply

HumV—High-mobility multipurpose wheeled vehicle

IMADET—Individual Mobilization Augment E Detachment

IRR—Inactive Reserves

KKMC—King Khalid Military City

LAI—Light Armored Infantry (also an armored vehicle)

LCAC—Landing Craft Air Cushion

LVS—Logistical Vehicle System
(also called Dragon Wagon)

MKT—Mobile Kitchen Trailer.

MLRS—Morning Launch Rocket System

MOPP—Mission Oriented Protective Posture (i.e., clad in chemical weapons protective gear)

MOS—Military Occupational Specialty

MPS—Medical Personnel Supply

MRE—Meals Ready to Eat

MRLS—Multiple Rocket Launch System

NBC—Nuclear-Biological-Chemical

NVG—Night Vision Goggles

OIC—Officer in Charge

PAA—Primary Assembly Area

PT—Physical Training

PVS-7—Night Vision Device

RD—Round

RPG—Rocket Propelled Grenade

RT—Radio Telephone

SAM—Surface-to-Air Missile

SAR—Search and Recovery

SIOPS—Psychological Warfare Operations

SMCR—Selective Marine Corps Reserve

TAA—Temporary Assembly Area

TAC—Tactical Air Control

TACC—Tactical Air Control Center

TOW—Targeted on Wire

VC—Vehicle Commander

VMP—Vehicle Mission Planner

Lt. Commander William H. LaBarge is a Navy carrier pilot based in San Diego, California, where he lives with his wife, Nancy. He is currently working on his fourth book, ROAD TO GOLD.

SHARE THE EXPERIENCE OF
DESERT VOICES
WITH YOUR FRIENDS AND FAMILY

Additional copies of *Desert Voices* can be ordered direct from HarperPaperbacks. Simply fill out the coupon below.

MAIL TO: HarperPaperbacks
                10 East 53rd St.
                New York, N.Y. 10022
                Attn: mail order division

Quantity:_____

ISBN: 0-06-100354-9   PRICE: $4.95/each

       Subtotal...............$_____

       Postage & Handling............$___1.00____

       Sales Tax
       (NY, NJ, PA residents).......$_____

       TOTAL
        (Remit in US funds.
        Do not send cash.)...........$_____

Name_____

Address_____

City_____State_____Zip_____

Allow four weeks for delivery.